Second-Wave Millennials

Tapping the Potential of America's Youth

WARREN WRIGHT

Foreword by Neil Howe

Second-Wave Millennials: Tapping the Potential of America's Youth
by Warren Wright

Published by
Second Wave Press
www.SecondWavePress.com

ISBN: 978-0-692-18041-9 (print)
ISBN: 978-1-7328685-0-2 (ebook)
Library of Congress Control Number: 2018911174

Editing: Cynde Christie, cynde_christie@yahoo.com
Book Design: Nick Zelinger, www.NZGraphics.com

10 9 8 7 6 5 4 3 2 1

First Edition

Printed in the United States

For Jennifer, Nick, Jackson, and all the generations that came before them and will come after them.

CONTENTS

Generational Wave Years

First-Wave Baby Boomers	1943 – 1951
Second-Wave Baby Boomers	1952 - 1960
First-Wave Generation X	1961 – 1970
Second-Wave Generation X	1971 – 1981
First-Wave Millennials	1982 – 1994
Second-Wave Millennials	1995 – 2004
First-Wave Homelanders	2005 - ?

Text conversation between GenXer dad and Millennial daughter

Want to go to the big game on Friday?

I'm down

Oh no, I'm sorry to hear that. What happened?

??

What?

omg dad really

No, really, why are you so down?

duh down means yes

Seriously? Huh.

FOREWORD

"Coaching is the new managing for Millennials." Warren certainly gets that right in his friendly, yet substantive, primer on how to lead younger generations in your workplace.

Time after time, I have listened to Boomer and Xer managers tell me what they think they know about Millennials: They have short time horizons. They don't care about benefits. They have no work ethic. They want to be left alone. They only want to be entertained. They're in it for the risk and excitement. They dress down to show disrespect.

And, time after time, I just end up shaking my head. Older generations get it so wrong.

Why? Because they keep thinking about what *they were doing and feeling* when they were young adults. They just aren't "woke" to the fact that every generation is different—which is surprising, when you think about it, since Boomers universally understand that they grew up having next-to-nothing in common with their own World War II-winning moms and dads. But apparently, what they clearly comprehend looking up the age ladder somehow eludes them looking down.

In this book, Warren lays out clearly so much of what older managers (a.k.a. "coaches") get wrong.

- In fact, Millennials have longer time horizons than older generations did in their youth. Most are sizing up career paths on their first job. On average, Millennials are starting to save for their retirement five to ten years before their parents even gave it much thought. And increasingly, they are looking for employers whom they can trust to provide them benefits that are *better* than just take-home cash.

- In fact, while Millennials do like regular work schedules: they are so prone to "work shame"—worrying that being seen as a slacker—that these young workers are letting roughly half of their paid vacation days expire, unused.

- In fact, Millennials dread being left alone. They want close and supportive relationships with managers, and they prefer to work collaboratively with peers. Entertained? No. Millennials want to be effectively taught—which means taught with the same immersive, online, and interactive tools with which they will be getting the work done.

- In fact, Millennials are the most risk-averse crop of youth to hit the workplace since their grandparents' generation. Across the board, indicators of risk-taking are down dramatically—from violent crime and teen pregnancy to tobacco use and drinking. Millennials tiptoe away from credit card debt, from buying stocks, even from marriage, before they have everything *carefully* in place. And when they dress down, it's almost never due to disrespect. It's because no Boomers or Xers in their lives—their parents or their employers—has ever given them any clue about the dress standards expected of them.

Mark Twain had it right, "It ain't what you don't know that gets you in trouble. It's what you know for sure that just ain't so." And Boomer and Xer managers know so many things for sure!

In this book, Warren untangles myth from fact by taking you on a journey across generational diagonals. He will show you clearly why age twenty-two or thirty-two to one generation can mean something entirely different to the next.

Yet, more than just awareness-raising, Warren takes you through actual solutions, rules, habits, and practices that can enable employers to get the most out of their Millennial hires. After telling you how to think differently about this new generation, he will tell you how to create a workplace that inspires and energizes them—that gets the most out of them while at the same time empowering them to get where they want to go in life.

Again, many of these lessons fly against ingrained generational wisdom—i.e., wisdom familiar to Boomers and Xers because it was true for them. When they were young, these older generations wanted less direction, less guidance, more individual incentives, more "space." Guess what? In most cases, Millennials want the reverse.

Many Boomers want to be the employer *they wish they had back* when they wore bell-bottoms in their 20s. Ironically, what Millennials want is more like the employer Boomers *actually had* back then. That concept flabbergasts today's older managers. But Warren makes the case well.

Warren also points out a useful and emerging distinction between Early and Late-Wave Millennials. He's referring here to Millennials who are born from the early 1980s to the early 1990s versus those born from the early 1990s to the early 2000s. The former, older group, who mostly have Boomer parents, are already well launched in their careers. The latter, younger group, who mostly have Xer parents, are still getting underway.

Every generation, as it ages, manifest interesting contrasts between its "first" and "second" wave. Early-Wave Boomers, born in the late 1940s, had more stable childhoods, got married earlier, and have done better in the economy than Late-Wave Boomers. Early-Wave Xers grew up with Atari and came of age with Reagan; Late-Wave Xers grew up with Nintendo and came of age with Clinton.

The emerging contrast between Early and Late-Wave Millennials should prove to be equally significant. Many of the trends we already associate with the early wave—toward sheltering, structure, teamwork, risk-aversion, and rule-following—are showing up earlier and more conspicuously in the younger late wave of this generation. This reflects, in part, the influence of their Xer parents and their post-Great Recession entry into the labor force. And, of course, the rising anxiety most Americans feel about their nation's long-term future.

In time, following these late wavers, we will notice a whole new generation. These will be the Post-Millennials. We call them "Homelanders." Employers aren't meeting them yet. But maybe they should start to put them on their radar screens. They're coming.

Finally, let me add that while I have been writing about generations since the late-1980s—wow, that's about thirty years! I have had the experience of advising employers who worry about generational change for almost as long. Over the last decade, I have the pleasure to work with Warren professionally as a workplace adviser and trainer. I can attest to the deep understanding he has developed and the savvy, hands-on, Gen-X-style of wisdom he has to offer. All of that comes across clearly in this book. I expect you will enjoy it.

Neil Howe

Three Generations Walk into a Room …

—— • ——

High up on the tenth floor of a brand-new office building in Las Colinas, Texas, just outside of Dallas, sixty-three-year-old Dave Winslow entered the lobby of his new place of employment with a look of supreme confidence. After a few years of forced retirement from his call center company, he was eager to get back in the swing of things. Retirement was no place for a man with a heartbeat. So long as he had one, he'd decided, he would be of use, not withering away on some La-Z-Boy with the tube on or playing golf five days a week.

It was mid-July, 110 degrees, and Dave was beginning to sweat through his button-down. As was his custom, he arrived twenty minutes early to what was supposed to be an introductory meeting. Sitting behind the desk in the lobby, a young receptionist smiled brightly. "Good morning. How may I help you?"

"Here for the meeting," Dave said, glancing around. "Eight o'clock." Dressed smartly in a white Oxford, a red tie, and slacks, Dave looked every bit the Baby Boomer he was. He'd woken up at the crack of dawn, shaved his face, shined his shoes, and cooked himself a plate of bacon and eggs and a big mug of Joe with time to spare for the commute. Growing up, he'd always been told, "The early bird gets the worm." Dave was here to get that worm.

With a nod of her head the receptionist indicated where he should go. "Conference room on the left. You're a bit early, but there's coffee and doughnuts on the counter. Take a seat, and the boss'll be right with you."

Dave gave a perfunctory smile. "Thank you, young lady." Then he headed into the conference room, whistling an old tune. He poured himself black coffee, took a plain doughnut from the box (he was watching his sugars), and sat in one of the uncomfortable office chairs at the back of the room. Scrawled in messy cursive on a whiteboard up front were the words, "Get to know each other!" Dave sat back with a frown, pondering its meaning.

Dave the Boomer had it pretty good. Starting out in the call center when he was twenty-five and fresh out of the Army, he quietly worked his way up the ladder until he eventually landed the SVP of Sales. He loved to tell everyone his story: How for over forty years, work had been the focal point of his life. He'd never shirked responsibility. Not once in his long career had he ever called in for a sick day. Never. Not even for the birth of his first child, his second, or even his third, for that matter. Work was life. Life was work.

He did, however, find time each year to take the missus to some tropical locale. They vacationed in the Bahamas, staying in nice hotels with pools and restaurants and golf courses. Everything they needed was onsite, so they didn't have to brave the streets for entertainment—they simply stayed at the hotel. It was a traditional existence he lived, one of home-cooked meals and big family reunions, of washing and waxing his red Camaro on Sunday afternoons in the sun, and having a beer with the boys on Saturday nights with the game on.

These were his hobbies, but all of them paled in comparison to his true passion, his true drive—work. This business was apparently a fast-growing software company undergoing a massive hiring spree. Dave had no doubt that within six months he would be meeting and exceeding the sales quota. He was sure of it.

There was a hurried knock at the door to the conference room, interrupting his thoughts. A woman in a dark blouse entered. She was in her mid-forties, her brown hair held up in a tight bun and an expression of quiet resignation in her soft blue eyes. She did not look happy to be there or unhappy; she seemed utterly indifferent. She smiled so quickly and disingenuously that Boomer Dave was taken aback. "Hi," she said dryly. "I'm Jennifer."

Dave reached out his hand. He was careful not to squeeze her fingers as hard as he would a man's. "Dave Winslow," he said, nodding left. "Coffee and doughnuts there on the counter."

"I'm fine, thanks." She sat down a few seats to his left, crossed her legs, took out her phone, and immediately started scrolling. Dave frowned and glanced away. *Yup*, he thought. Six months to top salesman. *This'll be even easier than I thought.*

At forty-four years old, Jennifer was a member of Generation X, the generation following on the heels of the Boomers and ending before the Millennials. Growing up in a time of rapidly shifting societal values, hers was also called the Latchkey Generation. In her time, divorce rates were high and adult supervision low. All her life, Jennifer had been harassed and discriminated against, held back from raises and promotions she'd duly earned. She was always much more capable than her job responsibilities entailed, but she didn't complain. Such was her plight.

Life was always hard—her parents divorced when she was a teenager, and she was raised by a single mom. As a young woman, her mom moved into her house and her dad died. Also known as the Sandwich Generation, Jennifer now had her own twelve-year-old at home, but since her husband was only making half as much as her and the cost of a kid (and a diabetic mother) was increasingly taking its toll, she'd been forced to take a second job: This one. Her new sales extravaganza. She hoped the sales commissions would improve her situation. But she didn't count on it.

She and her husband had bought their house at the peak of the market in 2007, and they were falling behind on their mortgage. She took this job not because she wanted to, but because she had to. In her heart, her dream was to open a restaurant in the south of France—Arles, perhaps, where Van Gogh lost his mind—and live out a quiet retirement. *Such were dreams though*, she reminded herself. And dreams often didn't come true.

At eight o'clock, a young man entered the room dressed in a fitted suit with no tie. His blonde hair was slicked back. A Starbucks cup in hand, he looked ready to take on the world. He smiled brightly and genuinely. "Hey, guys," he said with surfer-dude nonchalance, extending a hand to Jennifer, then Dave. "Josh Bartlett. How's everybody doing today?" There were a couple of polite grumbles. He nodded quickly several times, his voice strong and self-assured. It immediately irritated Xer Jennifer and further cemented Boomer Dave's belief that he would take over the place. "Cool, cool," Josh said, quickly taking a seat. Within seconds of sitting down, he was asking for their life stories, gauging them—trying to understand their purpose and values, secretly digging for what they brought to the table.

Clocking in at thirty-three-years-old, Josh was a First-Wave Millennial, meaning he was born during the first half of the Millennial Generation, whereas Second-Wave Millennials were born during the second. He was smart and capable. He could run circles around all his bosses, but over time he'd learned not to be too much of an overachiever because that meant far more work for him. He believed there were two parts to life: work and free time. He'd learned to separate them. When he'd first entered the workforce over a decade ago, he was eager and ready to take on any task, but over time, he realized that work is partly a political game, and he's just a pawn in a large game of chess. The Boomers around him were the anointed kings, providing only vague direction and praise, prone to long tangents during meetings about everything except work-related stuff, talking about their time on the golf course, their kids in college, their brand-new sports car, and their vacation at some sappy resort.

Growing frustrated with the atmosphere, he'd decided to take on a new gig. Although it was sales, rumor had it this was a pretty high-concept company with a relatively young CEO who did things his own way: not like the status-quo jobs Josh had bounced around in his whole life. This was something new, exciting, different, and he was more than ready to take it on. After years of becoming disenfranchised by companies where the senior management purportedly practiced some higher purpose, but in reality were lining their own pockets, he was eager to work with a company that did a healthy measure of both. The key word here being "with" because Josh didn't just want to work "for" a company; he had already done that. He wanted to be a part of something greater than the sum of its parts. Above all else, he desired purpose.

For the next ten minutes, Josh unknowingly annoyed both Jennifer and Dave with his constant friendly chatter and probing questions. Of course, Boomer Dave was no stranger to conversation, but usually he was the one dominating it. Given his seniority, couldn't this young man see the problem here? Wasn't he overstepping just a little bit? Boomer Dave sat back with quiet disapproval, nodding but tuning out everything Josh said.

Jennifer, on the other hand, simply wanted to get in and get out—to do her job adequately and not worry too much about having to make friends with her new coworkers. Truth was, she didn't care. And she didn't need any more friends. A twelve-year-old and a husband were enough as it was.

As the minutes ticked away, the three of them noted a strange feeling mingling in the room, an undistinguishable sense of tension. Still scrolling on her phone, or at least pretending to in order to look busy and therefore exempt from the conversation, Jennifer kept thinking, *Do I really have to work with these guys for the next however-many years? Ugh.*

Josh, now quiet with the wind struck from his sails, slouched far back in his chair, feeling vaguely uncomfortable for the first time since his arrival. After ten minutes of conversation, he felt zero rapport with either of his new coworkers. He chalked it up to being used to working around Millennials of late, not old fogeys like them. His survival instincts kicked in: if he was to progress with this company he'd have to stick close to the boss's side. Impatiently, he glanced up at the clock. Where was the boss, anyway? He tapped his feet rapidly on the floor.

Then, at 8:15, everything changed.

Someone new walked into the room, but it was not the boss.

Dressed casually in a black and white striped top whose hem stopped before the waist of her jeans began, revealing a thin strip of flesh that left Dave agape in outrage and Jennifer fighting the urge to roll her eyes, twenty-two-year-old Samanthe gave a nervous half-wave, bringing her hand up and then quickly thrusting it back to her side as though she was unsure whether it was the appropriate response. "Hi," she said uncertainly, her voice a little shaky. "I'm Samanthe."

Everyone gaped at her. "You mean," said Dave slowly, "Samantha?"

She shook her head politely. "Nope." Her eyes flitted from his. "Samanthe. With an e."

Dave raised an eyebrow, shrugged. "Well, that's a new one." He glanced at the other two for backup. Jennifer nodded in agreement. Josh said nothing.

"Are you, uh ..." Samanthe began, trying to find the right words, "the boss man?"

"No, young lady," said Dave sternly. "And I'd advise you not to call him 'the boss man.'" Samanthe blushed at this. Dave quickly added, "If it were me, that is. Just saying."

"Thank you ... sir." The word felt strange on the tip of Samanthe's tongue, like a drop of acid. No one had prepared her for this world. She'd grown up in a bubble of her happily-married parents' making: her safe-haven with its white picket fence and manicured lawn and her cookie-cutter high school and perfect college, where she hadn't even needed a summer job because her parents made her go to SAT classes. In fact, between basketball club, her summer camp volunteering gigs, and her triple major, she'd *never* had a job. Now here she was, day one at her first job ever, with people who looked at her like she was a lab experiment gone awry. She felt utterly, terribly alone—ill-equipped to be there. She nearly knocked over her chair when she took her seat.

Fortunately, Samanthe knew this job was a good one. In college, she'd learned that software development is the future. It's where the money is—where the growth is—where she can achieve great success. *I've got this!* she shouted internally over the voice insisting otherwise. She'd trained all her life for this—what could go wrong?

The air of unease in the room intensified, growing thick like fog in a horror film. It was as if each of them were in a spacesuit and suddenly the oxygen ran out. But they couldn't call for help because they dared not speak to one another for fear of feeling strange. A curtain of incomprehension descended over the conference room. All at once, they wanted to escape.

Though each of them felt their own sense of unease, none were more put-off than Samanthe. Dave, Jennifer, and Josh had all worked with different generations in the past. It was a necessary evil for them, and they'd learned to live with it. Though, if you asked, they couldn't really pinpoint how to work with the differences of their opposing generations; they simply understood there were certain differences among varying age groups, and—over time—they'd learned ways in which to avoid or work around them.

Dave liked to get to work early and stay late, and he expected the same ironbound work ethic of his underlings and peers. Jennifer was precise and efficient with her time, but she sure as hell would not be staying late, nor would Josh, who desired a purposeful gig even above money. They were each distinctly different, not just in age and appearance, but in experience. In mindset. In productivity. In technological proficiency and communication. Certain traits had been instilled in them upon the very moment of their birth, and that's not even to mention their own individuality.

These traits, above all else, are because of the time in which they were born. Dave, being a Baby Boomer, was born between 1943 and 1960, right at the tail-end of the greatest war the world had ever known and during or preceding the major consciousness revolution of the '60s. Those with no memory of World War II, but who benefitted from the resulting economic high, are Boomers. Each generation is made up of roughly twenty years. During the two decades following Dave's birth, he bore witness to the rise of America as a global superpower in the wake of World War II, the banging of Khrushchev's shoe at the United Nations, a man on the moon, the death of a beloved president, and the birth of the counter-culture movement. It was a time of free-love in Haight-Ashbury and a historic spike in birthrates, a rejection of traditional values replaced by diehard idealism. Boomers were taught by loving parents to work hard, to effect change, and to love thy neighbor.

Jennifer, on the other hand, received the backend of all that goodness. An Xer, she was born between 1961 and 1981, when parents were busy working. This is the generation no one talks about, the generation no one really cares about. Characterized as slackers, cynical and abandoned by their parents, Xers were quickly thrust into a world where they had to constantly look out for themselves. Even television picked up on the change. Disney's *Old Yeller* was summarily replaced by horror movies featuring evil children like the *Omen* franchise, *Children of the Damned, The Child,* and *The Children,* in which a nuclear power plant leak turns a busload of children into monstrous zombies with black fingernails who eat people.

Like many of her peers, the abandonment she experienced as a child had a lasting effect on Jennifer's overall makeup, not just in her personal life but also in her work life. Xers grew up learning to be skeptical of authority figures and archaic business principles. Whereas Boomers had an all-work-and-no-play attitude, Xers firmly established the work/life balance. Given their tendency to think outside the box, they're also natural-born entrepreneurs. They want their businesses and institutions to be run efficiently and productively. Arguably, they were also the first generation to fully grasp the rising technological shift in society, bearing witness to the ground floor of Apple computers, the World Wide Web, and software engineering. As such, they have grown to dominate the technology industry.

Then there are Josh and Samanthe, members of the largest generation in US history, the Millennials. Born between 1982 and 2004, this generation is so large and diverse, (and the coming-of-age experience of the older ones and younger ones so different) that social scientists, generation-watchers, and marketers are starting to make up new names for each camp. Many are now calling the older ones Xennials, as their characteristics seem a cross between Millennials and Gen Xers, and the younger ones Gen Z-, or Post-Millennials, as Pew Research calls them. But a generation is (by definition) the length of a phase of life, or about twenty to twenty-five years long. Bill Strauss and Neil Howe came up with the name "Millennials" in the 1991 bestseller, *Generations*.

Who comes up with the names and birth years of these generations, and how do they change? Well, there is no single authority on generations, but definitions and age brackets have a remarkable way of settling down based on the collective wisdom of the crowd. Generational naming is the ultimate example of long-term crowdsourcing. Consensuses on generational names emerge over time and usually settle themselves by the time the oldest of the new generation is in their 20s.

This book will separate Millennials into two distinct categories: First-Wavers (born between 1982 and 1994) and Second-Wavers (1995-2004). Though similar in some broad ways, these two groups vary greatly from one another. In Josh's home, you might see his vinyl collection alongside his floor-to-ceiling bookshelves, teeming with paperbacks of the classics, modern literature, and magazine subscriptions. In Samanthe's room (she still lives with her parents), the Kindle on her coffee table sits alongside her mini MacBook. She has all the books and music she'll ever need on two devices that can easily fit in her purse. Her universe is one of gigabytes and likes. Tweets and Snaps. This book is about Samanthe, not

Josh. Second-Wave Millennials are just now entering the workforce, and they're befuddling older generations in workplaces across the nation. The purpose of this book is to introduce you to who they are, how they think, and what you need to know in order for them to survive and thrive in the workplace.

Yes, Josh and Samanthe are both part of the Millennial Generation and share many of the same traits. They're both digital natives. They were both raised to feel special by their parents. They are both high-achievers who are pressured and stressed. They gravitate toward the idea of community and teamwork over self-reliance, and they have a strong streak for civic engagement. Finally, they are mission-minded and value the notion of purpose in their work. But the similarities end there. In this book, you will learn more about Samanthe and what makes her and other Second-Wave Millennials unique.

A First-Waver, Josh's upbringing was the antithesis of Jennifer's. He was loved, coddled, and protected from the ills of the outside world. Mom and Dad were always there for him, watching the news and warning him sternly about strangers in vans and outside of shopping malls. Growing up in the most ethnically diverse generation, he navigated multicultural environments with ease. He was less discriminatory than preceding generations—more tolerant of the LGBT community. Being a member of the most educated generation in US history, not only was he sensitive, he was smart to boot. He came of age in the 2000s, during 9/11 and the 2008 economic recession. He watched *Barney, Rugrats,* and then *Power Rangers,* and was labeled as confident, achieving, collaborative, civic-minded, and protected. Unlike previous generations, Millennials have a good relationship with authority. Their parents are their best friends, sometimes even shadowing them on job interviews.

Josh and Samanthe's was the first generation in history that had to distinguish between the first life and the second life, the latter being one's identity in the Digital Age: on Facebook, Snapchat, Twitter, YouTube, and online video games. On the backs of the technology crafted by Boomers and Xers, Millennials cultivated unique virtual selves.

Millennials are socially conscious. They understand that their purchases are in effect "votes." When they buy organic products and free-range meats, they're supporting their environment and taking a small part in subduing cruelty to animals. They're more socially conscious than any generation before them. All these traits mean one thing: Millennials are a new animal entirely. So new, in fact, that folks have a hard time trying to define them, let alone understand them.

Allow me to let you in on a little-known secret: generations, or the span in which we are born, define every aspect of our lives. They decide who we are, how we act, what our values are, and what drives us. One could even say having an understanding of a generation's coming-of-age experience provides a lens through which we see into the future, but that is a conversation for another time.

Suffice it to say, for decades the global economy has been steered by the hands of the G.I.s, the Boomers, and the Xers. To them I say, "Look out. Because you've got another thing coming: they're called Millennials." Through them we have the chance to unleash a workforce of awesome potential, one in which there are not only value propositions, but social consciousness. If you're reading this book, prepare to bear witness to the most revolutionary and civic-minded generation since the G.I.s: one that will surely change the world. They're already entering the workforce in droves, and soon they'll replace older generations as the de facto breakroom population.

But in order to utilize them to their fullest potential, first we must understand them, as well as the nature of the generational divide.

———— • ————

At 8:20 a.m., someone else walks into the room. Everyone looks up.

"Hey, guys," I say. "I'm Warren Wright. And no, I'm not your new boss. I'm your coach." In the ensuing silence, I sneak a glance at the whiteboard, at my handwriting. "So … did you get to know each other?"

Josh, Dave, Samanthe, and Jennifer look at each other, perplexed. Their expressions say, *guilty*. They just learned lesson number one: their judgment of each other put up a roadblock which made them forget the very purpose of their being here. They did not get to know each other.

I let out a gentle laugh, my hands up. "I didn't think so," I say, "but it's okay. Really. That's why I'm here. Over the next week, I'm going to teach you how to work together, irrespective of your age. I'll turn this team into an optimal sales force. It's not gonna be easy. You'll have to learn new things and unlearn a great deal of old things. But in the long run, it'll be worth it to your boss, to future managers, and to each of you. "Now," I say, walking in front of them, "are you ready to get started?"

Introducing the Generational Divide

——— • ———

Misunderstandings About Generations

Most people are uninformed about generations, yet they manage to gravitate en masse toward publications that reinforce their preconceived notions about younger generations (usually negative), including articles erroneously reclassifying and conceiving new generations and age brackets. As a result, there's a broad misunderstanding of the definition and length of a generation. When we talk about a generation, we're actually talking about a social generation—groups of people born over a period of time of between twenty and twenty-five years who witness similar economic, social, political, and cultural forces in their coming-of-age experiences. Because of these collective experiences, they share common traits and characteristics for the rest of their lives.

One of the reasons behind the misunderstanding of generations is that there's no central source of scholarly information on the subject. There's no trustworthy body of work people can go to for definitions and answers. There are just a lot of random social sciences in different areas that have their own views and definitions. You can't go to college and get a degree in generational studies because universities haven't embraced generations as a topic. The body of work that does exist on generational studies provides only surface-level information.

Kurt Andersen, a contributor to National Public Radio, wrote a book called *Fantasyland*. In it, he takes on the mantle of chronicling the history of the United States from its founding in the 1600s onward. The premise is that as time marches on, people believe in whatever they want to believe in, as opposed to the actual truth. This includes the topic of generations.

Probably the best research company that tracks generational trends, particularly in the last ten years, is Pew Research. Their framework for researching generations is built on the work of Bill Strauss and Neil Howe. Other than Pew, there are very few institutions dedicating themselves to generational studies. Many research organizations break the population up into age groups in whatever way is most convenient, but Pew actually follows the rules of generations. Pew treats generations as a force worth measuring because they know it's going to influence the future. They've accumulated massive amounts of data on buying behavior, marriage, and anything else having to do with human beings and how they interact with one another.

No one ever paid much attention to generations until Strauss and Howe wrote the definitive work of the same name in 1991. Until then, people didn't say the word "generation." The Baby Boomers were the very first to be documented heavily in the media. The Who's "Talking About My Generation" was a defining rock and roll song. By the time Millennials came around, media coverage of this generation reached new heights. You do a Google search for Millennials and massive amounts of information pop up, much of it wrong.

Generations in the Workplace

How many generations are in the workplace today? It's often said there are four or even five generations of people in the fulltime labor pool, but the answer hinges on the definition of "generation," and simple math. A generation typically spans eighteen to twenty-two years. Currently, 97% of the workforce in the United States is eighteen to seventy-three years old, a fifty-six-year spread, according to the US Bureau of Labor Statistics. That means it's unlikely you will have more than three generations in your place of business at any given time.

Right now, the generations in the workforce are Baby Boomers, the oldest of whom are in their mid '70s, Generation X members, and Millennials, the youngest of whom are just entering their teen years. Generation Z members or (as we prefer to call them) Homelanders are barely old enough to stay home alone. Although there are only three generations in the active workforce, the generational differences are significant. A survey of thousands of employees in the insurance industry, for example, revealed that three-quarters of respondents agreed there are important generational differences and those differences "sometimes" or "often" pose challenges in the workplace. These differences include how members of each generation set goals for themselves and others, what members of each generation want from their managers and coworkers, and even something as fundamental as how they communicate.

Generational Differences

These generational differences in the workplace can hinder productivity. This is an inevitable problem, but one with an easy solution. We could improve productivity if managers and team-leaders worked to foster an awareness of these differences, but unfortunately, they simply don't. The reason this problem is being ignored rather than treated is because most people aren't aware that generational gaps have anything to do with productivity. In fact, many would argue that's absurd. I understand their apprehension, but I believe I can change their minds.

In my consulting practice, I help each generation understand not only other generations, but also themselves. You'd be surprised by the powerful effect this sort of education can have on people. With an understanding of how they were raised and how their upbringing influences their behavior, people develop a self-awareness that helps them perform their best in every aspect of their lives, including work. Self-awareness manifests itself in effective communication. The way a Boomer and an Xer communicate with one another is different than the way Millennials communicate with one another. If people aren't aware of that and aren't flexible to the idea of communicating a little differently with people of different generations, productivity will drop.

Generational differences impact every aspect of the workplace. Each generation has a unique perspective of what work is and the role work plays in their life. Boomers, for example, put work very much at the center of their lives. They literally define themselves by their work. Before the Boomers was the Silent Generation and the G.I. Generation, for whom work was simply a means to an end. They had punch clocks; they punched in when they started work and punched out when they stopped. When Boomers came to the workplace, they blew all that up. "No punch clocks," they vehemently declared. "We're coming in early and staying late until we master this." The Boomers invented the workaholism epidemic.

Generation X looks at Boomers and says, "It's great you get in early and stay late, but what do you actually accomplish during that time?" Xers are into lean thinking, cutting out the middleman and doing things more efficiently to save money. Boomers want to build mission and be purposeful, and Xers just want to get the job done on time so they can go home and be with their kids. That's one of the things that's very different about Xers: They prefer to live a more balanced life. Xers are the first generation to introduce flextime workplaces, and they heavily influenced the working-from-home dynamic. They tend to compartmentalize their lives (work in one box and family in another), whereas Boomers lump everything into one big mission: work.

Then we have the third generation: Millennials. Millennials' attitude toward work is different from Boomers and Xers. Life is more important than work, period. "Work is great," they say, "and I want to work in something that has a purpose, where my unique talents can better the organization and accomplish a positive mission in the world. But my work does not define me. What defines me is me." Millennials prefer workplaces that offer flexibility, just like Xers. They want to fit their work into their life, not fit their life in around their work. Millennial rapper Drake, in his song *Motto*, proclaimed, "You only live once: YOLO," and ever since, YOLO has been the recurring, meme-infused creed of the Millennial Generation. Millennials say, "You only live once. This is my life; I'm not going to let work consume it."

Generational Differences Come to a Head in the Workplace

With their differing mindsets towards work, interesting dynamics present themselves. As a Millennial, Samanthe is a rule-follower, so if she read in the work manual she's supposed to start at eight a.m., that's what she does. She comes in at eight a.m. sharp and leaves at five p.m. sharp. Dave the Boomer scoffs when he sees her gather up her things and head out at five. *Unbelievable*, he thinks, shaking his head as he continues his work. He'll be there for another couple of hours, at least. After all, he just started this job; he has to establish himself.

Jennifer the Xer rolls her eyes at both of them. At this job. At everything. Samanthe notices and stops in her tracks, hurt.

"Um. Isn't it time to leave?" she asks Jennifer in a small voice.

Jennifer sighs. "Yes. Don't take it so seriously. It's just a job, you know."

Samanthe, though inclined to agree with her new coworker, can't help it—this is more than just a job. This is something she's worked very hard for. She sits back at her seat and opens her laptop, ready to work late. "I just want to do my best," she manages.

"Well, I wouldn't expect any attention if I were you. We're just here to get the job done."

"Maybe you should take your work a bit more seriously," Dave scolds roughly from across the partition. Jennifer smiles stiffly, unfazed. Confused and wildly uncomfortable, Samanthe carries on working, completely unsure if she's doing the right thing or not. She feels utterly adrift, as if she's disappointed someone, but she has no idea why. Again, she just wants to do her best.

The poor Millennial is so confused in today's Boomer and Xer-dominated workplace, they don't know how to effectively do their job. They're balancing the ideals of two very different preceding generations with their own. Then they came to work, where they were thrust into a hodge-podge of different expectations: a world in which there was no clear set of rules.

Optimizing generational relationships at work requires each of the generations to grasp the mindset of the others. To do this, we need to understand not just the traits of each generation, but the stories behind them. Every generation has a place in history—a story influenced by the social, cultural, political, and economic factors that shaped them. There are countless experiences in day-to-day life that shape a person into who they are, but few as influential and far-reaching as a persons' generational coming-of-age experience. Generational differences are one of the most influential, yet undervalued, dynamics in the workplace.

So We're All Different. What's the Issue?

The workplace is truly a one-of-a-kind environment. It's the one place where you're thrown together with random people from different generations and told to work together. Of course, there are many places where intergenerational experiences happen, like within families or at church, but there's no place except work where you all have to work together to complete a project with varying, and often sharply contrasting, views on how it should get done.

When generations don't recognize the others for who they are, their hot buttons and motivations, then engagement suffers. Research has shown repeatedly that if someone doesn't feel committed to what they're doing, they're not going to be productive. In other words, when engagement suffers, productivity is adversely impacted. And when productivity suffers, people quit or are laid off. This turnover is costly and has far-reaching consequences on the economy and society at large.

Higher engagement levels within a company create more value for that company and the customers it serves. If you aggregate the collective value of several companies, you are impacting the overall economy. When I worked at the managing consulting company Gallup, we were able to track engagement levels at a nationwide multichain retail store and correlate the data to value in the form of customer satisfaction, productivity, and profitability. Our consultants and researchers discovered that teams with high employee engagement rates are 21% more productive and have 28% less internal theft than those with low engagement. If you extrapolate that dynamic with the rest of the economy, while realizing generational differences affect the value of a company, this has a profound effect on the fate of our economy. Perhaps you went into this thinking generational differences were a small matter, but the reality is that our ability to better understand the mindset of each generation has effects far beyond a single company.

Communication

To tackle an issue this large, we have to shift the focus to communication. We all know communication is the foundational element of any relationship, and the method (email, text, or verbal) we use to communicate matters. Each generation has their own perspective on how a piece of information should be communicated. For example, when a Boomer or an older Xer receives an email from a Millennial, they expect that email to be grammatically correct and the punctuation to be perfect. There should be one idea per paragraph. It should follow the rules of writing. But Millennials are changing the way written communication is done.

Dave, Samanthe types, *I finished the product review- Wat r ur thoughts?*

This isn't accidental; the way Millennials communicate is quite sophisticated. They incorporate emojis and abbreviations and acronyms, which is a pretty effective way to communicate. So no problem, right? Not if a Millennial is communicating with another Millennial. But if a Millennial is following those rules of communication with a Boomer or an Xer, they're immediately going to be discounted. The Millennial will suffer for their way of communication. Dave thinks, *She's not very bright—she can't even spell.* But for Millennials, spelling is not the point. As long as you get the idea across clearly, then you've communicated effectively.

"Jennifer," Dave whispers. Jennifer looks up from her computer. "Look at this." She walks around to Dave's computer to read the email. She laughs.

"I can't believe they're letting these kids into the workplace," Jennifer says. "What a waste of time."

"It's not funny," he grumbles, shaking his head. *The world really is going to hell*, he thinks.

Jennifer is mildly amused, but mostly just wants to get back to work. "Whatever," she says as she leaves Dave to read and reread the nonsense Samanthe sent him: *Hey, did u guys fill out the report yday?*

I've interviewed some highly successful older Millennials, and they text with their clients all the time, day and night. It works well with their Millennial clients and a lot of their Xer clients, but it does not work for their Boomer clients. A Boomer client is likely to think, "That's an invasion of privacy, sending me a text at ten at night. Who the hell do you think you are?" A Millennial, on the other hand, is more likely to think, "Awesome. The guy representing me is so dedicated, he's working at night on my behalf!"

Method of communication is not the only difference between generations. Every generation has its own "communication attitude." This attitude is reflected in their behavior. Think of it this way: Each generation has their own slogan. For the Boomers it's, "My way or the highway." The implication in the workplace is, "I'm the boss, and you're going to listen. It doesn't matter if you like what I think or not." Boomers do not mince words. When they have something to say, they say it. There is not a lot of gray area for Boomers; it's a black and white world.

Xers have a different philosophy of communicating. Their slogan is the iconic Nike, "Just Do It." Unlike the Boomer, an Xer is okay living in that gray area. After all, they are a generation accustomed to making sense out of a topsy-turvy world. However, they like to find their way out of the gray area so they can accomplish their task for the day and get home to their kids. Xers mostly just want to get shit done. They work quickly, they work efficiently, and they stay on task.

The Millennial slogan is "friend me." Millennials don't want to disappoint anyone. They're cautious and risk-averse, not as direct as Boomers and Xers. They'll dance around issues and drop hints, but they're not ones who look into the face of the Boomer and say, "You've pissed me off." Sometimes that means they lack the courage to stand up and say what they think because they don't want to offend anyone. This sensitivity can translate to misunderstandings. For example, a Millennial may think their boss is being outwardly mean, when, in reality, he's just trying to help.

I'll give you an example with a manager and a Second-Wave Millennial. I know a man who manages a popular chain restaurant. "You gotta help me out," he told me one day. "I hired this seventeen-year-old server and on her first day of training she had shoes on that weren't comfortable. When you're a server, there's a certain kind of shoe you should have. So I tell her, 'Those shoes won't work. We have some we can recommend.'"

Later he overheard the girl say to a friend, "The boss is so mean. It's day one, and already he's making me change my shoes!"

The boss wasn't trying to be mean; he was trying to help. He knew her shoes were going to make her life hell. I told him, "Next time, focus on her specialness."

He frowned at me. "Say what?"

I told him: A feeling of specialness is one of the seven primary characteristics of Millennials. They're raised to feel they're central to their parents' lives and the lives of all the adults around them. Instead of being so blunt—so black and white—my friend should say with a kind smile, "Jessica, I'm so glad you're here on our team."

"Aw, thanks, Jeff."

"You bet," he says. Then, leaning in almost conspiratorially, "Hey, can I give you a word of advice?"

She leans in, curious. She already got a confidence booster, so she's more open to accepting advice. In fact, she wants it. "One of the things that really helps people get better at this job is comfortable shoes," Jeff says. "We've got a clothing catalog with the perfect kind. All of us here wear them. How about you order some, try 'em on, and make sure you're comfortable with them. What you do you think?" You should always ask for their feedback. This shows them they're in a democracy, not a tyranny. Their opinions matter.

You can guess what the results would be. On the flipside, what are the ramifications of Jeff's initial reaction? Jessica might become resentful towards Jeff and fine-tuned to his later communication "misdeeds." Over time she may grow dissatisfied with her job and quit. Jeff will have invested hundreds of hours in an employee's training, who now leaves and needs to be replaced, starting the process all over again.

Millennial Engagement

The core characteristics of Millennials are: special, sheltered, confident, pressured, achieving, collaborative, and community-oriented. We can hone our communication style to those main characteristics. Part of the purpose of this book is to provide a framework for how to behave in the workplace. Everybody has their own way of doing things, but there are some basic principles, things anyone can do as a manager to foster productive and effective communication and encourage productivity in your workplace.

I want workplaces to become better for everyone: The company itself and everybody who works there. I want people to show up to work excited to be there and engaged in what they do. Helping employees understand the various generations and their perspectives raises engagement levels. Remember, that's our ultimate goal: *to raise engagement levels.* That's the dependent variable we're trying to change. And understanding generations is the first step towards allowing that to happen.

The Three Levels of Engagement

At Gallup, I was able to work closely with Dr. Jim Harter who, along with Curt Coffman and Marcus Buckingham, were among the first to define employee engagement in their best-selling book, *First, Break All the Rules.* The three levels of engagement were: **engaged, not engaged,** and **actively disengaged.**

An **engaged employee** puts discretionary effort into their work. They are psychologically committed to their job and their company, and they will put in extra effort voluntarily.

You can just look at them and tell they're enjoying their work. A **not engaged** person is coming to work and doing their job, but there's not a lot of effort beyond what's required for the job. They're just getting the work done. It's a means to an end. The third category is **actively disengaged**, comprised of employees I like to call "work terrorists." They run around causing trouble because they're so miserable. Their misery is like a plague, and they spread it to each person they come into contact with. Their hatred for their work makes them want to ruin everything about it.

Gallup has measured engagement levels for over ten million employees and, although the numbers vary company to company and year to year, generally about 20% of the US population is engaged, 60% is not engaged, and then another 20% is actively disengaged. There are many factors that can influence engagement, but the biggest is the manager. Maybe you're completely committed to the mission of the company, but if you don't get along with your manager, you're still going to become disengaged, or even actively disengaged, and eventually leave the company.

The Effect of Collaboration on Engagement Levels

Another interesting dynamic that can affect engagement and productivity in the workplace is collaboration. Millennials tend to be fairly collaborative, more so than Boomers and Xers, so when you give Millennials an individual assignment, or God forbid you compete them against other Millennials, they don't like it. They'd rather work in a group to accomplish the task, using the software that's out there to help people collaborate, like Slack, and even being compensated in teams. Without collaboration, Millennial engagement will fall.

Xers, on the other hand, come from a place where competition is a part of life and, although some may collaborate, it's in their generational DNA to resist teamwork. The thinking goes for Xers that you either make it or you don't, and no one's going to help you. Often, when I walk into companies where an Xer is the CEO, I can just *feel* the competitive spirit in the air. It's palpable. In these environments, particularly sales environments, the dog-eat-dog mentalities rule: you win, someone else loses. In these environments, Millennials feel lost. They value a friendly, positive environment. The culture of an organization is important to them—a culture that is collaborative and affirming. Outside of an environment like this, they may feel disenfranchised and unheard, and certainly disengaged.

Five Ways to Craft an Ideal Workplace for All Generations

Every now and then, an article comes out by a consultant or journalist that emphatically states generational differences are a myth, and that all employees want the same thing from their company. There is now a mountain of research by Pew Research, the Annenberg Foundation, Harris Interactive, National Center for Educational Statistics, University of Michigan Institute for Social Research, Gallup, Zogby, UCLA, and dozens of other reputable organizations that all contribute to the growing body of research about generational differences. Most credible researchers no longer debate about the validity of generational differences, but, at the same time, there are some core things all generations share about what they want in an ideal work environment. These five principles are typically present in great workplaces for all generations.

1. A good leader, whether they're an Xer, a Boomer, or a First-Wave Millennial, is authentic, purpose-driven, and self-aware. If the boss can make those values a priority and is open in their communication style, then they're going to set the tone for a productive workplace. Good leaders are honest about who they are. They are authentic. Since one's identity is in part one's generation, a good leader embraces the strengths of their own generational characteristics. High self-awareness helps the leader understand their own blind spots, as well as the strengths of those around them.

2. From leadership flows the **culture** of an organization. The notion of culture is elusive and often overlooked, even though it is the very air that employees breathe in their workplace. I often draw analogies between an organization and the human organism. A healthy organization, like a healthy person, is fit, resilient, stable, and usually in good relations with those around them. A sick organization, on the other hand, is weak, vulnerable to harmful outside forces, and potentially rotten from the core. The book *Culture Eats Strategy for Lunch*, written by my friend and former Gallup colleague Curt Coffman, states, "Strategy is a promise that culture must deliver." Inspired from a quote by management guru Peter Drucker, the book outlines how to spot a great culture and what drives it. All generations want to work in a positive-culture environment where their skills and talents are recognized and allowed to soar.

3. Professional development and self-awareness are integral to a good workplace. In a healthy workplace, there is a concerted effort to value the diversity every individual brings to the table and to help others recognize the diversity of others. There are many tools out there that can help with this, like StrengthsFinder or the Emotional Intelligence Assessment. In my consulting practice, I use an assessment for managers called *What's My Coaching Style* from HRDQ that helps managers better understand their inherent strengths as a coach. Most people are aware by now that professional development is a huge priority for Millennials, more so than previous generations. Regardless of the generation though, all employees deserve to be recognized for their unique strengths.

4. Just as individuals should be recognized and valued for their diversity, good companies **develop platforms that work** for all generations. Unfortunately, there is often reluctance to embrace new systems. An example I often see in companies, which is now a huge source of generational tension, is regarding the new collaboration software Slack. Millennials overwhelmingly line up for Slack and its easy, open, and inexpensive format, while Boomers line up against it, claiming it's not secure and compromises the company's system architecture. A lot of times, older generations push back against these platforms because they've always done things another way, which has worked well enough. But they have to adapt in order to accommodate the new generation of employees.

5. Great working relationships increase productivity. While culture may be the whole body, great working relationships are the coordination of the organs that make up a healthy body. Ideally you would actually care about the people you work with and build a caring environment. You would openly accept errors and mistakes as part of the job and be forgiving of them. I've been in work environments that are tense, where you can't say the wrong word or write an email a certain way for fear of consequences. All these angry rules make it easy for employees to fail. No one likes an environment like that.

Second-Wave Millennials

There's a lot to be said about the effects of generational differences in the workplace and how we can learn to communicate better, but the larger purpose of this book is to introduce Second-Wave Millennials to the world. I'll describe their characteristics and how they vary from older Millennials and from all other generations. Then I'll provide tools with which you can manage them to be happy and productive workers, so your company can thrive.

Of course, the Second-Wave Millennials themselves are the real benefactors of this book because they will be managed better, their engagement will go up, they'll stay with companies longer, and they'll be more satisfied with their work. They'll finally be understood. Unfortunately, very few older people today really understand Second-Wave Millennials.

Second-Wave Millennials are grappling with all these new dynamics of the work environment. *What's appropriate to wear? Do I have to use a phone? Can I text my boss, my client? How do I navigate workplace culture?* These are some of the daunting issues faced by young people when they walk into foreign environments completely different than school, where people are using lingo they don't know and looking at them sideways. Facilitating an understanding of these young adults will help not only them, but us as well.

The Big Picture

The fact is that generations affect the way we live our lives every day. People continuously underestimate the role generations play in shaping human history. Take the G.I. Generation, born between 1901 and 1924. They occupied the White House for thirty years, won nine presidential elections, and produced seven presidents. The G.I.s were known as a generation of leaders. They were builders and makers of institutions that still stand today: the United Nations, the International Monetary Fund, and the World Bank. They won a world war, crafted the Marshall Plan, built the nation's highways, and championed bold programs like The Civil Rights Act. It's no coincidence that it all happened under the leadership of this generation.

By contrast, look at the Silent Generation, born between 1925 and 1942. According to author Frank Conroy, "We had no leaders, no program, no sense of our own power, and no culture exclusively our own. We were ... silent." The Silent Generation did not put forward a single president. They were, however, "skilled arbitrators, mediating arguments between others—and reaching out to people of all cultures, races, ages, and handicaps" (from *Generations* by Strauss & Howe, p. 282). I don't want to leave the impression that some generations are bad and some are good (although I can say some are luckier than others). For Silents, leadership simply wasn't their thing.

A Silent would say, "We can't compete with our G.I. parents, so we'll just get in line and be the good citizens our parents always wanted us to be."

After the Silent Generation came the Boomers, and (of course), their imprint on society is still being felt today. They changed the way we dress, the music we listen to, the language we use, and championed civil rights and feminism. They now preside over the most dramatic and destructive culture war our country has seen in several decades.

Every generation has an indelible imprint on how we live our life today. But it is always the newest generation that confounds and perplexes all other generations the most. We now ask of the Second-Wave Millennials: *Why do you act that way? How did you get like that? What are you thinking? Finally, What will be your indelible imprint on our society?* Allow me to set the framework for people to understand them. But to understand them, first we must discover why generations matter.

Why Generations Matter

——— • ———

By definition, a generation is a group of people born over a twenty to twenty-five-year period who share coming-of-age experiences like social norms, economy, politics, and pop culture. Those broad categories tend to be dominant factors influencing a group of people at any given time. The collective group of people influenced by them exhibit traits and behaviors similar to one another and that carry through into the rest of their lives.

Like I said, generations are a driving force in the historical narrative of the human race. Sounds dramatic, but it's true. It's people from a generation who start wars or don't start wars, create economic policy or abolish it, direct social norms or upend them. A generation decides how they want to raise *their* children, who, through that experience, decide how they raise their children. For example, after twenty-plus years of Xer neglect, a moral panic ensued, and as Millennials were being born, there was an enormous shift towards more hands-on parenting. Innumerable books came out on the topic.

The generation with the highest percentage of employees is typically the culture that dominates the workplace. When I started consulting work on generations, many organizations I worked with only had 10-15% Millennial employees. Now Millennials represent 30-35% of the workforce, and the culture is changing in the way all generations change culture when they hit a level of dominance. Generations matter in the workplace because they affect everything about it. Let's start to look at each of the generations and how they behave differently in the workplace.

An Intro to Baby Boomers

I assume you're buying this book to understand how to better manage Second-Wave Millennials, especially in the workplace. So, you're probably asking yourself: *Why do we need to talk about Boomers and Xers?* Because knowing the background of previous generations, we have no context for what "Millennial" really means.

Boomers are a fascinating generation. Their archetype, according to the Strauss-Howe generational theory, is "prophet." Prophet generations are often associated with cultural or religious revivals, rediscovery, and reawakening. In the late '60s, there was a popular concept that music could set you free. If you're an Xer or Millennial, you're like, "What the hell does that mean?" Here's what it means: for the Silent Generation, life was conformity. Life was going to work, raising a family, pursuing a career, and being a good citizen—conventionality. Everybody looked the same, dressed the same, and talked the same. As you can imagine, life was pretty boring.

Then Boomers came along and said, "Fuck that. We're going to wear tie-dye, grow our hair long, and do drugs. How do you like me now?" Music was used as an expression of this rebellious spirit. Boomers then took a systematic approach to dismantle the very system that made them, doing everything they could to take themselves away from the conventionality of life. They're very good at breaking systems; they've always been a generation that breaks things, outsiders criticizing the mainstream. The irony about Boomers is that now they are the mainstream, but they continue to break things from the inside out. Look at government and politics today—it's all a mess. Who do you think is in charge now? Boomers. They were better as a generation when they were breaking down barriers in civil rights and feminism.

In his book *The Innovators*, Walter Isaacson wrote about innovators in the last 100 years in the United States. He writes about Steve Jobs and Steve Wozniak, a couple of hippie geeks living in the Bay area who developed the personal computer in their garage. Before that, the only existing computer was the size of a gymnasium. Computers were huge mainframes run by large corporations like Sperry Rand and the government, structured and corporate. Computers were a part of conventionality, part of the system. No other generation would've invented the personal computer; it had to be the Boomers.

It wasn't just the technological prowess at the time or the need to innovate, though that certainly was a big part of it. Much of the development of the personal computer had to do with the ethos of the Baby Boomers at that time. They wanted to unhook from the grid in every possible way, including computers. They wanted to stick it to the man, poke conventionality in its all-seeing eye. So, naturally, they developed a computer for themselves.

Everything Boomers do, they do big. In the '60s and '70s, they protested the Vietnam War and the Nixon administration and effected social change on a massive scale. We actually talk differently now because of Boomers. We dress differently. They're the arbiters of culture. Take a look at what's popular on Spotify: the music Boomers created is still the most popular music. There's a lot of music out there, but classic rock will never die.

They're a crowded generation. There was no bigger generation at the time: that's why they're called the Baby Boomers. When they got to work they broke that system too, changing it to fit them. They made work central to their life. Doing it big, just like they do everything big, they invented workaholism. The notion of coming in early and staying was never done before the Boomers came along. They set the precedent. If you read deeply into the Strauss-Howe theory, you'll learn there are dominant and recessive generations, typically every other generation. Boomers are dominant. Xers are recessive. Millennials are dominant. Homelanders are recessive.

An Intro to Generation X

The term "Xers" didn't come about until Doug Coupland wrote a book called *Generation X* in 1991. Doug was a perfect case-study of Generation X. Born in 1961, he grew up in a broken home, had divorced parents, and was very lost. He even spent some years literally wandering the desert. Every generation has a story, and the story of Gen X is parents stopped paying attention to their kids. It's like the free-range generation. Birthrates dropped to all-time lows and abortion and drug-use rates were at all-time highs. According to the CDC, risk behaviors, like not wearing seatbelts and drinking and driving, were at an all-time high, as were crime rates. There was an overall sense of hopelessness and cynicism. The reason Doug named them Generation X is because it was the generation that meant nothing. No labels. Just "X."

Think about the Woodstock song Boomers Crosby, Stills, Nash, and Young wrote. "We are stardust. We are golden … and we got to get ourselves back to the garden." Remember, for Boomers it was all about mission and purpose. But then look at the lyrics of Soundgarden, Green Day, Nirvana, and all the grunge bands Xers grew up on. Many have a much more negative message: "Don't wanna be an American idiot. Don't want a nation under the new media. And can you hear the sound of hysteria? The subliminal mindfuck, America."

Creep by Radiohead sets the tone of a person who feels they're not useful and never will be. Nirvana made a lot of money with the song *Suicide*. The culture was completely different. Stacks of "evil child" movies came out between 1964 and 1987: *Children of the Corn, Rosemary's Baby, Chuckie.* Children were seen as devils. This all fed into the running narrative of the unwanted child.

Let's fast forward. How do you think that plays out when they become adults? They're actually the most entrepreneurial generation. Why? Because taking risks is something they've done all their lives. No one's ever watched out for them. So, what do they do? Start a company. Two companies. Ten companies. Failure is normal, after all. They've failed all their lives in the collective eye of society. They figure, "What the hell? I'll give it a shot." Xers are risktakers. They experimented with drugs even more than Boomers, believe it or not, and much more than Millennials. For Xers, there's a gravitation towards risk. That's why Jeff Bezos and most of the top Silicon Valley entrepreneurs are Xers.

In the technology sector, you usually hear Boomer names. We hear about Bill Gates and Steve Jobs, both Boomers. But no one knows who the two founders of Google are. I always ask during my presentations, "Does anyone know the two founders of Google?"

Do you?

Sergey Brin and Larry Page, both Xers, are in charge of one of the largest companies in the world, one you use every day, but you're not familiar with their names. Xers weren't paid attention to as children, and they're still not paid attention to. But what spawns from that is a self-reliant generation used to picking up the pieces and dealing with difficult times.

When you go through your formative years with low expectations about how you are to be treated by the people and institutions around you, you develop a high tolerance for … almost everything. Boss doesn't recognize you for a job well done? Yep, didn't expect that anyway. Become caught in the crosshairs of a company downsizing? Sure, it was just a matter of time. Boring and repetitive job? Hey, it's a paycheck. Failed miserably at that task? Been there before. I'll just bounce back and try again. Gen Xers didn't get trophies or gold stars when they were kids and do not expect them as adults in the workplace. Xers are the least whiney generation—with the possible exception of whining about how entitled Millennials are.

Being an Xer myself, I'd like to share with you some of the remarkable strength and resilience of this generation as it relates to the workplace. First, Xers tend to be innovative because innovation requires repeated failures and resets. Xers' greatest learning came from trial and error, and in many ways, failing and picking yourself up again and again is a key component of innovation. As Thomas Edison said, innovation is 1% inspiration and 99% perspiration. Innovation also happens because it has to happen. If a project needs to get completed on time and the existing system of operations is insufficient to meet the challenges, an Xer will reinvent a new system in order to meet the required timeline. As the saying goes, "Necessity is the mother of innovation."

But not all Xers are running around innovating all day. Some are just doing the grunt work because that's what has to be done. Xers may not be loyal to a boss or company, but they typically are very loyal to the task and the outcome that is expected of them. Some jobs are boring, some jobs are challenging, and some jobs involve high-stake political maneuvering. Whatever the case, Xers have become remark-ably adept at handling any type of situation that is thrown at them. They are not fragile. You cannot easily hurt their feelings. And this brings up another positive aspect of Xers at work—the time it takes to manage them. They do not need a great deal of supervision. They just like to know from their boss what the goal is and then have the boss get out of the way. Want to motivate an Xer? Tell them, "I don't care how you get it done, just do it—and, by the way, we don't do long meetings here."

As bosses, Xers value efficiency and cost-control. They tend to watch the bottom line very closely and are not afraid to make tough decisions, including risky moves in strategy and operations. For all the work they do, however, Xers demand a work/life balance. Xers are exceptional at compartmentalizing their lives. During the day they're a hard worker, in the evenings and weekends a doting parent, and (occasionally) a binge-watcher of *The Blacklist* or *Shameless* with their Xer spouse. Remember, these are the helicopter parents, or as I like to call them, Jetfighter Parents, raising their Second-Wave Millennials. Yes, they will complete a project, but nothing is going to get in the way of their daughter's soccer match or son's karate tournament. After all, they'll need to leave work early to go to the trophy shop first.

An Intro to Millennials

Compared to the wild ride of the '60s and '70s, Millennials were born during a culturally and politically stagnant time. Defined by the social shift that happened in the late '80s and early '90s, when there was a dramatic increase of parental involvement in the lives of children, they're sometimes called "spoiled" and "coddled." In their youth, we started seeing "Baby on Board" stickers on cars. It's when Chrysler came out with their minivan, which is basically a vessel for the baby. Vans used to be like dens of iniquity; the Xers used them for drugs and sex. By the time Millennials came along, parents were buying vans to keep kids safe. Talk about a value-shift.

There was an enormous movement by parents towards protection to combat the growing sense that kids were out of control. It was like an epidemic: Crime was high and education levels were dropping. Basically, when Xers had children, their rebellious side took the backseat, and protecting their children took the front seat. The birth of Millennials was the death of Xers, in a way, which fits into the narrative of the cycles of generations in history.

Because Millennials were always paid attention to, what emerged was an overall feeling that they're special. Contrary to popular belief, that's not necessarily a bad thing. "Special-ness" often gets conflated for entitlement. When you're raised with a lot of attention, getting to work and realizing you don't have that attention anymore is a shock. With Xers it was like, "Oh well, no one pays attention to me anyway, so I'm just going to figure out how to do my job." Millennials don't think that way. They come to work with the expectation of having their needs met, and when they aren't, Millennials grow dis-satisfied.

Hands-on parenting also led to an embracing of teamwork and collaboration in Millennials. Millennials were raised by Barney the Dinosaur, who used to say, "I love you, you love me, we're a happy family." Even the cartoons coming out when Millennials were young were oriented towards cooperation, collaboration, and solving problems together. The cartoons when I was young were Tom and Jerry, which were a mouse and a cat constantly trying to murder each other in new and exciting ways. Imagine that shift. Millennials' icon was a purple dinosaur that said, "Let's work together," and the Xers' was Oscar the Grouch, who lived in a garbage can in gritty Sesame Street, just getting by. Even the way these characters speak has strong implications.

The other thing going on with Millennials was that parents expected a lot of them. They expected them to accomplish big things. As a result, Millennials are obsessed with achievement. They have to know they're going somewhere great. School systems started tracking student performance more carefully, and school funding went up because there was a social demand for it as people realized they needed to help kids achieve.

This heavy focus on achievement in their youth has carried into Millennials' lives today as well. At work, they want to accomplish things to the highest degree, and their Xer manager looks at them like they're nuts. "Just slow down; chill out. You've got to put your time into it," but the reality is most of the time Boomers spent was just waiting for the right opportunity, which approached them frequently. They got promotions very fast because the GDP tripled when they were coming of age and entering the workforce. With an economy growing that quickly, both jobs and promotions were plentiful. They got jobs easily out of college. Millennials have always had to compete with one another, and there's a shitload of high achievers for them to compete against. It's harder to get into college, harder to get a good job. A bachelor's degree isn't enough; you need an advanced degree to get the job you want, and you need several internships too. All that is an extension of the focus on achievement, which continues today.

Similarly, Millennials are also rather risk-averse. Drug and alcohol abuse and abortion rates were all extremely high when Xers were being born. When Millennials were born, all that went down. Today abortion rates in teen girls are 70% lower than they were in the mid '90s. Millennials don't do a lot of drugs, and they're not having a lot of sex. They're not engaging in risk behaviors, and the reason goes back to that protective helicopter parent watching over them closely and expecting achievement.

Like Boomers, Millennials tend to be mission-minded and purpose-driven. They want to derive meaning from their work. Their view towards work is, "Life first, work second. I want my work to actually add to the purpose of my life." Their parents always guided them towards finding something meaningful, but it also has to do with their notion of civic engagement and involvement. Millennials volunteer at higher rates than any other generation in history. They are more likely than any other generation to help someone in need. They're more likely to buy products and use services that help the environment and contribute to more sustainability and a better world.

"Watch Out, Generation Z is Coming!"

Or so the media would have you believe. But the reality is this so-called "Generation Z" is not yet entering the workforce, and, in fact, has barely reached puberty. Most social scientists who track generations say the first people born from Gen Z were born between 2002 and 2005, making the oldest fourteen, and the youngest ... not yet born. Generation Z is a "default" name given to the generation that followed "Gen Y" (more widely recognized as the Millennials), which itself was a follow-up to Generation X. But the naming of generations was never meant to be an exercise in sequencing the alphabet.

We call the cohort born after Millennials "Homelanders." We call them this, in part, because they are literally at home more than previous generations. Studies show that this generation does not go outside and play as much as previous generations, instead playing video games and doing homework, staying safe under the watchful eye of their helicopter parents. Another reason we call them Homelanders is the geopolitical mood sweeping the globe right now. From Russia to China to right here in the US, there is more focus than ever on keeping the homeland safe and distancing ourselves from far-flung alliances. Homelanders will be growing up during a time when we are looking more inward and are less likely to welcome outsiders. This is the generation that will be coming of age in a post-Brexit global environment.

With the oldest Homelanders barely old enough to mow the lawn, you won't see them shaking up the workforce anytime soon. The fact is, it's simply too early to be talking about their influence on our world in any significant way. Most companies are still trying to master the Millennial mindset.

The Four Turnings

The Strauss-Howe theory posits that there are four different "turnings" within a lifetime, each about twenty years long. The first of the four turnings is called The High. The High is a time of rebirth and renewal, of building and possibility. During this time, society tends to be very confident and institutions strong. People believe in what they can accomplish individually, but mostly they believe what they can accomplish as a group. During first turnings, families tend to be connected. Ideals are established and settled, and there's commonality around ideals, unlike today. In first turnings, institutions are reinforced. There's not a lot of breaking going on. Social structure is unified and the worldview is simple. The social priority is maximizing community, and the social motivator is shame. You don't want to step out of line, and you want to do everything as a group. The vision of the future is bright. If there are any wars during the first turning, they're restorative.

In the second turning, The Awakening, institutions begin to be questioned and attacked. There's a lot of passion for culture, but social structure is starting to splinter. Families are starting to weaken and break apart. The social priority, instead of community, is rising individualism. This is the consciousness revolution; the Baby Boomers came about during a second turning. The sense of greatest need is to fix the inner world, not the outer world. It's about personal spiritual growth.

During this time, there's still a bit of positivity about the future, a little religious zeal, and euphoria. We can see that in the drug-induced blur of the late '60s, where the idea was to build a new Garden of Eden where everyone could live communally and peacefully. Though there are elements of community, at its core, this turning is about the individual in his or her own LSD state. Wars in the second turning tend to be fairly controversial, like Vietnam. Should we be there? Shouldn't we be there? Who the hell knows?

The third turning is called an Unraveling. During the second turning, people thought institutions were too strong and started attacking them. By the third turning, institutions are eroding. They start ossifying and getting desiccated, and they no longer function well. Culture becomes cynical. The

Boomers had this idealism about a greater world, but Xers' vision of the future was very dark. Crime rates, drug-use, and abortion rates were at record highs. Things were falling apart. The social motivator was guilt. The social priority was maximizing individualism. You had to watch out for yourself, not your neighbor. But if you're not watching out for your neighbor, you're not going to build a community. The antithesis of community was unraveling. Wars during third turnings are inconclusive, such as in the Middle East.

Then we enter the Fourth Turning, the Crisis, which is what we're in today, in 2018. It started around 2008 and will continue until about 2028. In the beginning of a Fourth Turning, institutions have eroded. We could have expected in a Fourth Turning to see Donald Trump elected president. When he was elected, everybody started calling the author of *The Fourth Turning*, Neil Howe, and saying, "Oh my god; it's happening. The Fourth Turning is here."

A Fourth Turning is comprised of four parts: catalyst, regeneracy, climax, and resolution. The catalyst was the economic crisis. I don't know if we've hit the climax yet. I think we'll see it within the next two or three years. It may be a large-scale cyber war or a nuclear war, something people are paying close attention to now. Only in a Fourth Turning would people even consider doing something so stupid, but that's exactly when things like this happen. We have this incredible erosion and almost collapse of everything we hold dear, but then remarkably, resiliently, out of the rubble and ashes comes something brand new. This is when new institutions start to be conceptualized and replace old ones.

Remember, in a First Turning institutions are reinforced, but in a Fourth Turning there's nothing there, and we're starting from scratch. We're creating a new world. The last Fourth Turning ended with World War II, the Paris Peace Treaties, and the United Nations.

It's my belief that government will be remade in the eyes of the Millennial Generation. That's who is going to reestablish the founding of our society and governmental systems because they see things in a more technology-focused way, in a more practical way, in a way that's grounded in what's good for the community. We're going to see them come out in elections and change the way we vote. Millennials are now running for local offices like mayor. They'll increasingly hold offices at the federal level beginning in the 2020s. They'll migrate into the national scene and reshape culture, society, politics, and government. There will likely be a rising-star Millennial, perhaps another generation of the Kennedy clan who will lead and rebuild. The sense of greatest need for Millennials right now is to fix the outer world. The vision of the future is urgent.

Taking a look back into the last three centuries, Fourth Turnings climaxed with major wars: the Revolutionary War (1775-1783), Civil War (1861-1865), and World War II (1939-1945). They are all about eighty years apart. In each case, without exception, an economic collapse, a disintegration of social order, and a declining institutional effectiveness preceded these wars, while a new civic order and institutional effectiveness, along with economic growth, followed them. We can trace these repeating patterns all the way back to the 1400s.

Why Do They Matter?

This is why: See how generations influence the way we live our lives? Generations are not hot topics on a day-to-day basis. They're not taught in the school curriculum or in colleges, where they might have the greatest impact. One of the most profound lessons these turnings teach us is to take the time to step back and look at history—step back and see what happens, how it happens, why it happens, and how it informs our future. But our institutions don't really support that idea. When you go to college, what do you learn? You learn your subjects, but are you looking at the big picture? A meta-system of interrelated disciplines? Not really. It's a massive flaw in the evolution of humankind. We repeat the same mistakes over and over again. We repeat the cycle. The question is, can we learn from these cycles and actually improve upon them? Can we learn from our history, or are we doomed to repeat it? The best way to gain a knowledge-base and a framework for understanding the future is by studying cycles. We seem to be getting into wars every eighty to eight-five years: life-changing, world wars. We just repeat what we've done in the past.

Generational Traits Last a Lifetime

When I worked with Neil Howe at LifeCourse, one of our clients was a major hotel chain. They were investing many millions of dollars building new hotels, and we were advising them to think about designing in a way that's attractive to the next generation. Right now, the hotels are attractive to

Boomers and Xers because that's who's doing business travel. But in ten years? Millennials will be the dominant traveling businesspeople.

During our talks, the company asked us an important question: "When a twenty-five-year-old Millennial reaches forty, what are they going to be like?" Talk about a head-scratcher. The traditional answer would be, "A forty-year-old in fifteen years is going to be the same as a forty-year-old now, the same as a forty-year-old in the past. A forty-year-old is a forty-year-old." But that's a very static way to look at the future and anticipate the consumer needs of a particular demographic. For example, we know that for forty-year-olds today, it's important to have a quick check-in time. The fastest way to their room, the better. They don't want to mingle. They just want to get to the room, make sure the heat's working, and sleep. That's an Xer thing.

The assumption is that when a Millennial turns forty, that's the way he's going to be too. It's not true. The forty-year-old Millennial is going to be very much like the twenty-five-year-old Millennial. In fifteen years, that twenty-five-year-old is going to have the same characteristics. For example, we know from research that when Millennials do business travel, they would rather have a smaller room. They don't care about room size. Boomers and Xers want a big room. The assumption is everybody who's forty wants a big room. Again, it's not true. When Millennials turn forty, they're going to want a small room, so get ready for it. They'd rather spend more time in common areas. Hotels are changing. You'll notice if you walk into hotels there are more common areas, more open space. There's Wi-Fi. There are latte machines. That's because forty-year-old Millennials are not going to change into forty-year-old Xers. They will remain who they are.

Forecasting with Generations

As previously mentioned, and in an almost terrifying fashion, having a firm understanding of generational theory supplies a lens through which we can view, and even predict, the future. Columbia University has done an immense amount of work on party identification. Are you Republican or Democrat? One of the things they found that people just can't believe is someone's political party affiliation when they're twenty years old is typically the same as when they're in their forties and fifties. The common narrative is that people get more conservative as they grow older, and there is some data that says they may, but not by much. Neil and I were hired by the Congressional Institute, a Republican-supported organization, to do a study on the future patterns of the Millennial electorate. We found that Millennials are over-whelmingly—like we've never seen in US history—Democratic and progressive.

Republicans said, "We're not worried. They'll grow up and become more conservative." But they won't. They're going to be as progressive at forty-five as they were at twenty-five. Republicans are going to lose thirty years' worth of elections, and the entire political landscape is going to be realigned. This is big news, but not yet on the radar of the political pundits.

Understanding Generations

Improving our everyday lives? Not really. But understanding generations can help us with something we do every day. You guessed it: work. Understanding generations can resolve conflict and discrepancies in the workplace. In anthropology and sociology, one of the premises is that people work better in groups when—are you ready for this?—they understand each other better. What we're really doing by helping people understand generations is helping them understand the people they work with. There are a lot of ways to do that and many tools out there that can help, like StrengthsFinder, a strengths assessment developed by Gallup. After you take the assessment, you're provided with your top five strengths. If you understand yourself better, and if others can understand you better, then you can work more effectively together.

The assessment groups people into certain types. Some people are activators. Activators love to start things, but don't really like to finish things. They tend to be very entrepreneurial. They move quickly. Time horizons are short. If I'm in a group and people don't know that about me, they're going to look at me like, "Dude, what's wrong with you? You're moving too fast. Slow down."

On the other hand, there are those known as deliberative. Deliberative people are extremely careful about every decision they make and tend to move at a slower pace. I always made sure when I was at Gallup that my assistant was deliberative because I needed somebody to slow me down. There's also birth order. Are you the firstborn, second-born, or last born?

That affects your personality and behavior as well. Generations are just one more lens through which we can understand ourselves and others. Sadly, it's a lens no one really uses.

Implicit Biases

One unfortunate reality is that all existing generations view incoming generations negatively, in the workplace and in general. The new kid never lives up to expectations. As an Xer in the workplace, what happens when a Millennial comes to work for you? Without even talking to them, you already think they're not good enough. Boomers thought the same thing when you came to work for them all those years ago. It's called unconscious bias or implicit bias. We all come into the world with implicit biases.

"Ugh, this girl is going to slow us way down," Xer Jennifer mutters to the young woman who sits beside her.

"Samanthe?" the woman asks, sounding slightly offended. Jennifer looks up to find that the girl looks to be about the same age as Samanthe. Shoot … maybe she shouldn't have said anything.

"Well, you know how new hires can be … slow. And she just seems … young." Jennifer doesn't mention that she happens to technically be a new hire herself.

The girl shrugs. "She seems nice to me."

Jennifer sighs. "Nice" is not what she was talking about. This is a workplace, and things need to get done. Nice doesn't get things done. Jennifer watches Samanthe out of the corner of her eye; she's staring at her computer screen, a crease furrowed between her brows. Jennifer frowns. *The kid is probably scrolling through Facebook,* she thinks. *And who's going to have to pick up her slack? Me.*

In reality, Samanthe is going over the employee manual, trying to learn her responsibilities. We don't want to be prejudiced against people of different ethnicities than us, but we are. We don't want to be prejudiced against Millennials, but we are. This is why it's so important to foster a conversation around generational differences and strategies we can employ to create a more productive environment among them.

At the end of the day, you want a happy, healthy workplace where people are communicating effectively, where they're not holding back, and where they feel comfortable and trusted. You can't have that unless you understand fundamentally what people's generational orientation is. The principle of a good manager is to find out where your employees are coming from, how they think. You have to get to know the people who work for you, and understanding generations will help you do that.

Baby Boomers: *"My Way or the Highway"*

——— • ———

Boomers, born between 1943 and 1960, live by the slogan, "My way or the highway." They challenge rules and authority. They're individualistic, idealistic, and hardworking, traits that began early in their coming-of-age experience.

When millions of soldiers who served in World War II came back from Europe, Eisenhower built freeways and suburbs, and they settled down and had a lot of kids. That sudden spurt of population growth was aptly named "the Baby Boom." It was the largest generation in US history by population.

The defining point between the Silent Generation and the Boomers is the Silent Generation remembers World War II, whereas Boomers don't have any recollection of the war. What they do remember are the tremendous economic and social changes happening after the war. The GDP quadrupled between the end of World War II and the early '70s. It was a time of great economic progress and consumerism. By the time Second-Wave Boomers were being born, they were being raised by the Silent Generation. There was a lot of conformity, as the Silent Generation likes. We had TV shows like *Ozzie and Harriet* and *Father Knows Best*, where the men come home from work and the women have their meals ready for them. There was a system, a perfectly orchestrated normalcy about life. Boomers were raised in an environment in which they were taught they could do anything. They were the first entitled generation, the first "me" generation. Parents viewed them as little adults, and as a result, they were given a lot of authority at a very early age.

Raised in a consumer-friendly, peaceful setting where their parents earned more money than previous generations of parents, Boomers grew up comfortably. They didn't face the challenges of wartime, and (due to coddling families and a thriving economy) they were bestowed with a sense of great purpose. This was during a time when media and consumerism were blowing up. Madison Avenue was on fire. Washing machines and blenders were being sold en masse, and kitchen cabinets were being filled with food. Coca-Cola became a dominant brand. Andy Warhol made his famous tomato soup can piece representing the weirdness of over-consumerism and conformity. Amid all this, the Boomers finally said, "You know what? All this conformity is bullshit. It's time to change the way we live our lives. Everything that's going on in the world is wrong."

This was exemplified in *The Graduate*, a movie that defined the Boomer generation. The protagonist, Ben, graduates from a prestigious four-year school, and his parents throw him a pool party where Ben is approached by his dad's friend, who happens to be a prominent executive. "Ben, I just want to say one word to you. Just one word."

Do you remember the word he said?

"Plastics."

"Plastics" was a code word for an emerging industry in which you could make a lot of money. You could have a career and benefits, get married, and have kids. The course of your life was predetermined by that single word. A Silent Generation and G.I. Generation member might have responded, "Sign me up, sir!" But what did the Boomers say? After saying he'd consider it, Ben walked away, getting into his scuba gear and going to the bottom of the pool, silently sinking.

Haight-Ashbury and the Summer of Love

At the epicenter of the Boomer coming-of-age experience was a street corner in San Francisco called Haight-Ashbury. Often called the birthplace of the counterculture movement, it drew people from all over the country. A social commune based on the counterculture movement's ideals, outsiders were attracted by various drugs, psychedelic rock groups, and poetry readings. The corner was visited by such a vast influx of people that by the end of 1967 the streets were ridden with homelessness, hunger, and widespread drug abuse. A mock funeral called "The Death of the Hippie" took place in which the organizer of the event, Mary Kasper, said, "... this was the end of it. Don't come out. Stay where you are! Bring the revolution to where you live." Which is just what people did.

Boomers came of age amid the purveyors of culture. They said, "We're going to change everything," and they did. They started as the good kids of the suburbs. They were in The Mickey Mouse Club. Based on their place in history and their archetype, they quickly moved away from conformity and towards rebellion. Then there was a significant breakdown in government. Richard Nixon was lying to America. When the Boomers saw that, they declared, "This is a problem. This has got to change." The circumstances were a perfect stew for Boomers to resist authority.

My mother took me to a protest march of Nixon's inauguration when I was ten years old. There were two million people in Washington. I saw a guy get his head bashed in by a cop with a club stick. Talk about a defining moment. Today, sure, there are protests, but Millennials are very orderly about things. Back then it was wild, and Boomers were at the forefront.

One of the priorities for Boomers was rising individualism. *Forget about the suit. I'm not getting in line or following the herd. I'm going to do my own thing.* Places like Esalen in Big Sur, California became the epicenter of individualism and discovering the self through things like transcendental meditation. It was all about getting in touch with yourself. Unlike today, the focus was not giving back to the community and being part of the team. That's not what Boomers were about. They were about an inner world, not an outer world. Do a bit of LSD and go deeper, so you can be a better person. Remember pro-drug psychologist and writer Timothy Leary? "Do what feels good." That was the mantra. "Let the music set you free."

Rid the Enemy

Boomers have always thought there's an enemy out there, something from which they needed to liberate themselves.

When they were young, they were fighting the conventional enemy through traditional warfare. Today, Boomers are running the US government, and they're still fighting, only now it's with each other. They have deeply value-oriented beliefs that go beyond practical considerations. In Congress, they're not negotiating with the other side, they're just sticking to their own predetermined beliefs. When Ronald Regan and Tip O'Neill from the G.I. Generation disagreed, they would go out for a drink and work out a deal. The government doesn't work that way anymore because for Boomers there are two sides and no gray area. Boomers have always hated establishment. Now they are establishment, but challenging rules and authority is a habit they still can't shake.

The Indulged Generation

Boomers were raised as integral to the lives of their parents, who truly believed they could accomplish anything. This grand idealism is reflected in a classic Coca-Cola commercial of the time. A song called *I'd Like to Teach the World to Sing* played as everyone climbed up a hill to triumph together.

Millennials were raised in a time of idealism too, remember? Their parents built them up until they truly believed there was no one like them, and that they were really capable of changing the world. But here's the difference between Millennials and Boomers with respect to their idealism. Remember, Boomers grew up in a time of economic prosperity. They didn't have to worry about paying off loans, getting a job, making rent, or figuring out when they're going to get out of Mom's basement, all of which are very real problems for

Millennials. As a result, Millennials have a practical edge. They have the practical elements of Xers and the idealism of Boomers, which makes for a powerful generation. But we'll talk about that later.

Boomers never really had to worry about getting a job because the economy was doing so well when they were young adults. They just migrated into idealism. There's a well-established longitudinal study by UCLA in which they interview freshmen at 400 colleges every year. They've been doing it since 1969. They ask the same questions, so you can see exactly what changes over time. One of the questions is, "Is it more important to have meaning in your life or to have a practical job?" An overwhelming margin of Boomers said it was more important to have meaning in life. When Xers were freshmen in college, the response flipped. The new consensus became, "I've got to have a job. When I grew up, the economy was shit. I can't afford idealism." Boomers wanted to focus on idealism, the notion of something greater. Problem is, they never could find the tools to get there. "We are stardust. We are golden. We've got to get ourselves back to the garden." That sounds all well and good on paper, but what's the plan of action, Boomer?

Boomers at Work

If you ever want a mission statement written for your company, hire a Boomer to do it. They're great at it. Just don't ask them how they're actually going to get there, how they're really going to accomplish that mission. That's the Xers' job. It's strange because Boomers are hardworking, so why do they struggle to achieve? Well, everyone is motivated by something, and Boomers happen to be motivated by the belief that they can make a difference. When they got into the workplace, they used work as a pretext for accomplishing their idealism, for getting behind something and really putting their mastery into it.

A big reason Boomers work hard is because they want everyone to know they're working hard. For the Silent Generation and the G.I. Generation, you checked into work with the punch clock, and then you checked out of work at the end of the day. You came when the workday started and left when the workday ended. Easy-peasy. But Boomers wanted to master work. They were going to let everybody know they had it under control. They were going to break rules, come in early, and stay late. But they were *not* going to wear a tie.

Everybody talks about Millennials being confident, but we forget that Boomers are very confident. Plus, they've been around for a while, so they're really not interested in other people's opinions. They're not natural consensus builders. Millennials are always asking, "Am I doing this right? Is this right? What do you think?" Boomers don't do that. They take individualism to the extreme. In the workplace, they will demand of you as much as they think they demand of themselves. In meetings, they tend to go off topic and opine about things that may not be pertinent. For me, being an Xer, it's frustrating to listen to a Boomer's story about something that may not be relevant to what the meeting is about. Often, it's about them or what they did or lessons they've learned. Of course, not every Boomer is this way, but I think many Xers and Millennials will have this experience with a Boomer.

Mentorship occurs in every organization, as it should, but viewpoints on mentoring are very different depending on the generation. A Boomer thinks mentoring is, "Let's sit down, and I'll tell you some stories. I'll tell you about my first day and what I focused on. Sit and watch what I do until you know how to do it right, and then I'll take you out for a drink and tell you some more stories." That's mentorship. "Get to know me. Through knowing me, you can understand what's going on." But Millennials want a step-by-step process of how they can improve the job they're supposed to do. Sure, they want stories. They want encouragement and advice. But mostly what Millennials want is the map they can follow to be as successful as possible. These are two totally different views. Boomers behave in ways that don't resonate with Xers or Millennials, and vice versa, and this goes for everything, not just mentorship.

Boomers take great pride in their work and tend to be loyal and committed employees. They focus on mission and purpose, which has real value. Not to mention, due to their age and loyalty, they've been around for a while. They have a lot of experience. We can learn a lot from a generation that's been in the workplace for a number of years. They'll likely transfer that loyalty to the people around them. There are many ways in which Boomers set a positive example for younger generations in the workplace.

However, they don't excel in consensus building. The opinions of others are not of high concern for most Boomers. They often exercise oversight over new ideas because they're set in their ways. Because they have high self-esteem, they tend to think their way must be the right way. The problem in the workplace if you have a stubborn attitude is that it shuts down collaboration. Culture comes from the leader, and if the leader doesn't encourage collaboration, then the entire system will begin to think and behave in the same way. Unfortunately, many Boomer bosses create an environment in which the employees serve the leader. The reality is those businesses will fail because they're not adjusting to the subtleties and dynamics of the marketplace.

Boomers absolutely must learn to adjust to the changing marketplace. Take communication, for example. Communication is key to any workplace. Boomers' emails, and conversations in general, tend to be very long—longer than they probably need to be. Knowing this, if a Millennial knows their Boomer boss has lunch at 12:30, will schedule the meeting at twelve so they won't have to spend hours listening to him talk. Xers agree with Millennials on this one: Boomers need to get to the point already. To other generations, Boomers often seem to be wasting time that could be used more productively.

Boomers and Millennials Working Together

Boomers and Second-Wave Millennials both value praise, but there's one big difference: with Second-Wavers, you have to be specific. With Boomers, you could just say, "You're fucking awesome," but Second-Wavers want praise that teaches them how they could do better, not that simply satisfies their ego.

What any incoming generation tries to do is mirror the behavior and culture of the generation in positions of leadership.

Millennials will do the best they can to adapt, to try to modify who they are and how they operate to mirror whoever's in charge. That's no easy task because it's not who they are or the way they want things to work. For example, Slack, a team-building software service, is popular among Millennials and can be very useful in the workplace. But Millennials can't just go to Boomers and outright suggest the company introduce the software. Boomers have always done just fine without Slack, and they're sure as hell not going to start using it now. Millennials have learned that in order to foster any progress in Boomer-headed workplaces, they have to make a business case, which they're great at. They go into it relaying the time and money Slack could save.

"By the way," the Millennial might add, "We've been using it for weeks, and it's nearly doubled our productivity."

A Boomer appreciates a Millennial breaking the rules like this because it reminds them of themselves. Boomers broke the rules all the time when they were growing up; they were always innovating.

"Oh … well, it looks like you've made your case!"

Millennials have to straddle this fine line between satisfying the ego of the Boomer and coming up with a logical solution to a problem. It's confusing to be a Millennial in the workplace and navigate a Boomer boss. It's not easy. But the reality is, today the youngest Boomer is fifty-seven. In five years, there are hardly going to be any of them left in the workplace. That means there's going to be much less interaction between Boomers and Millennials at work and much more between Xers and Millennials. Very soon, a new environment will emerge.

Generation X: *"Just Do It"*

— • —

The youngest Xer is probably thirty-eight years old. I'm an Xer, so I can't help but speak from an Xer perspective when I talk about this generation—and all generations, come to think of it. I'm a First-Waver, born in 1961, when the very first Xers were born.

Sometime in the late '60s and '70s, the Silent Generation parents decided there was too much attention on children. *Children should just be children; Why are we spending so much time on them?* Society shifted away from the adored, indulged child to the child with much less attention, and before long children were being completely ignored. Xers were expected to fend for themselves. There was very little supervision.

In the meantime, what was going on in America from an economic standpoint was a combination of high inflation and unemployment. If you wanted to buy a house in the late '70s and early '80s, the interest rate was 16%. People forget how high interest rates could go; it was completely out of control. The economy went from a boom to a bust as the Xers were coming into the world and becoming young adults. In the late '80s and early '90s, there were 1,800 people murdered in New York City a year. Right now, it's just 300 murders a year. Kids were doing a lot of drugs; cocaine had made its way to the suburbs and crack wreaked havoc in the cities.

According to the CDC, risk behaviors were at an all-time high with this generation. Almost 50% of high school students were smoking cigarettes. To put that in perspective, now it's 6%. It was a dangerous world they lived in. This led a lot of people to call Generation X the Forgotten Generation, the Unknown Generation. It got to the point where politicians and people in governance were saying, "These kids are feral. They are completely out of control." This eventually led to all the protection policies that Millennials actually embrace.

As the Xers came of age, their priority was survival. Think about it: As kids, they saw murders and drug abuse happening all around them. Forced to figure out a way to navigate the world without parental involvement, they adopted a self-sufficient, competitive attitude. Just look at Wall Street: it's mostly Xers. For Xers, workplaces were battlegrounds. They had to beat the person beside them. Kill the competition. It wasn't about collaboration; it was about winning. This mindset was reinforced through the Reagan administration. Reagan was very free-market-oriented and competitive, and as Xers became adults, they grew to be competitive, pragmatic, and practical. The Boomers were all about meaning, but the Xers didn't have time for meaning. They just wanted to find a job. It was about survival.

They trusted no one as they grew up, especially not the government. They were very negative. But, where Boomers always fought establishment, Xers simply ignored it. Boomers wanted to change the world, and Xers just wanted to change the channel. They watched their older brother and sister Boomers with big idealistic aspirations accomplish nothing. As an Xer myself, I remember saying "whatever" a lot.

GENERATION X: "JUST DO IT" | 83

When a parent scolded me, "Hey! Don't do that."

"Yeah, whatever."

An employee in the breakroom: "Jimmy didn't show up for work again today."

"Whatever."

The teachers: "Go to school."

"Yeah, whatever."

I have three older siblings, all Boomers. Even before knowing about generations, I always knew I was different from them, but I could never figure out why. When I was young, we took a family trip to Puerto Rico, which was unusual because my parents didn't spend money on anything. They were First-Wave Silents who grew up in the Great Depression and, as a result, were very frugal. In Puerto Rico, we all navigated the ocean's big waves. My philosophy as a nine-year-old was: *If you don't want to get involved, just get under the wave.* Don't ride the wave, just get under it and avoid it—let it pass over you. Meanwhile, my brother and sisters laughed at me. They were storming into the waves like battle-hardened Spartans. I didn't know it then, but it was the perfect analogy: Generation X likes to opt out, and Boomers don't understand that.

Gen X is largely uninvolved in civic life. A surprisingly high percentage of Millennials compared to Xers are in government right now because Xers simply never fully got involved in civil service; they went to Wall Street or became lawyers or tech entrepreneurs. They wanted to compete and win. The environment in which Xers grew up forced them to find satisfaction not in collaborative environments, but competitive ones. They're self-reliant. In fact, Xers are the most entrepreneurial generation in US history. The Boomers may have started Apple and Microsoft, but who actually made money on it? Who actually brought it to the marketplace? Xers. Xers will gamble and take risks at a higher level than any other generation. As a result, they've become the dominant entrepreneurs.

The Entrepreneurial Generation

Xers want to avoid the rules, change the channel. They don't want to fight the rules because they know there's no point in that. They watched the Boomers try and fail in that regard. The people around them aren't going to help, and they're not going to accomplish anything together. Entrepreneurism is the perfect endgame for Xers. It breaks the rules and takes them away from collaboration, from having to work according to the regulations of others. It's every man for himself in an Xer's head.

For Xers, there's work and then there's life. Where Millennials love to bring those two together, Xers make sure to keep them separate. Millennials want purpose for their life. They will work as hard as they can if it involves something meaningful. Xers see work more as a gig, a stop along the way. They want to go home and spend more time with their kids than their parents spent with them. That's what led to them becoming the overprotective parents of Millennials.

Xers at Work

Their parenting style varies greatly from their work ethic. Focused on efficiency in the workplace, Xers introduced the notion of lean thinking and cutting out the middleman. They don't waste time on mission statements. They spend their time cutting costs and making tough decisions. In the workplace, Xers have always valued self-reliance, adaptability, and efficiency. Whereas Boomers will work long and hard at perfecting a project, Xers spend their worktime figuring out the fastest way to get the most results so they can get home to their kids. They're looking to redesign things to save time and money.

Frankly, at times Xers may not have the vision necessary to be a CEO capable of moving a company forward because they're so focused on the details. That's going to be problematic in the future as Xers take over positions of leadership. Right now they're primarily middle managers and upper-middle managers, but as time goes on, more and more are beginning to take up the mantle of CEO. A perfect example of how an Xer behaves in the workplace is the current CEO of Microsoft, Satya Nadella. He took over from Bill Gates, a Boomer, a few years ago. In typical Xer fashion, the very first thing he did was lay off 18,000 people.

Xers won't overwork. They won't come in early and stay late. They'll do things as efficiently as possible so they can get back to their life. They don't tend to be as mission-oriented; they see work as a job. This may have something to do with the fact that Xers are the first generation to work without pensions. Pensions ended with Boomers. Defined benefit pensions meant when you retired, you'd get paid a percentage of your salary for the rest of your life. Now there are Xers who will be retiring with nothing. In fact, many will likely never retire because they don't have enough money. Boomers may be the last generation able to retire.

When I give presentations about Xers in the workplace, Xers love it more than anyone because I'm finally recognizing them as a generation, something no one ever did. A lightbulb goes off when they hear me talk about these traits: efficiency, functionality, self-reliance. This is who they are. Every Xer is different, of course, just like everyone else, but (like all generations) they certainly share commonalities. I think Xers bring to the workplace a sort of reality check. Let's say a company is run by a Boomer who really believes in the mission and underlying principles of the organization. He believes in the business model. An Xer will take a thorough look at it and announce, "Your business model is fucked." They're not afraid to say that.

Unlike Boomers, Xers are flexible and willing to change, and because of that, their companies will survive in the future. Managing is hard, and an Xer manager is willing to make tough decisions because they're used to facing consequences for their actions. If a company needs to cut 15,000 employees, the Xer will do it. A Boomer would be more hesitant, but an Xer is going to step up and do what needs to be done for the survival of the company. A Boomer might say that's bad because people are losing their jobs, but the Xer is looking to ensure the long-term sustainability of the business model, not to be the good guy.

The Future of Xers and Millennials Working Together

Coming back to one of their strongest traits, self-reliance, Xers don't really value mentorship. I certainly never had a mentor. As a generation, there was just never much focus on mentoring. And because Xers never had mentors, they in turn don't know how to mentor Millennials. Because they're a representation of their coming-of-age experience, Xers believe it's better to figure stuff out on your own in the workplace. Just do it. The idea of developing a person long-term, of spending time with someone who works for you and acting as a mentor, is foreign to Xers.

But here's the dilemma: Boomers are going to start retiring and Xers are going to take their places of leadership. When Boomers hand over the keys to Xers, there will be lots of differences in the way companies are run. I think there will be an embracing of contract employees. This is already happening in companies all the time, but I think it will become the norm with Xers. The reality is, if you hire a contract employee, you don't have to pay them benefits. It's more efficient. It's cutting costs. And we know how much the Xers love that.

I also imagine the idea of a gig economy will become more common with Xers in charge. A gig economy is the notion of people having many different jobs. Under the Xer-dominated regime, a person who contracts may do backend analytic work on Google, drive an Uber, and have a consulting practice on the side. As Xers move into leadership positions, there will be a further embracing of the gig economy, which is going to have a massive backlash. Millennials want more benefits, mentoring, and feedback, and Xers are going to cut that stuff out of the program. Here we have a clash of values.

I think what Millennials will appreciate about Xers is their stark honesty. Millennials have a practical streak in them, particularly First-Wave Millennials. They see things as they are, to a large extent, even though they're mission-minded and purposeful. They'll likely appreciate the fact that Xers can be real and make tough decisions in an organization.

A perfect storm is brewing: Xers already have an orientation for creating more efficiency, and then we have the advent of artificial intelligence and robotics. We're potentially looking at mass unemployment. Xers have always been a generation of haves and have-nots, so cutting employees and introducing A.I. likely wouldn't faze them all that much. No generation has had a wider disparity between people who make a lot of money and people who don't. The G.I. Generation introduced the idea of the middleclass, that we should bring the income toward the middle. Then Xers came along and blew that up.

A LifeCourse survey showed that 70% of Millennials trust and look up to the Boomers and Xers who work around them. Parents have served as role models to Millennials, and they have a strong bond. Millennials naturally gravitate towards and trust authority figures. Establish a formal mentoring program in which you act as a coach. Carefully identify good mentors through a screening system, and establish specific objectives and goals for the mentors. It's best to have a system that's monitored and measured, and if mentors hit their goals, they get a bonus. When you train a Boomer to be a good mentor, all of a sudden the Millennial becomes much more engaged. When done effectively, mentoring benefits all parties involved. I did a survey of a number of companies a year and a half ago, and the number one thing Millennials felt was missing in a company was good mentorship.

An Xer Boss and a Millennial Employee

A relationship between an Xer boss and a Millennial employee might be a little dysfunctional. Many Xers harbor disdain for Millennials, especially Second-Wave Millennials: disdain and confusion. Second-Wave Millennials are foreign to them. In 2018, according to the Lancet Journal, the premier medical journal, scientists within the fields of medicine, psychology, and sociology have raised the official age of adolescence from nineteen to twenty-four. That means by definition the Second-Wave Millennials coming into the workplace today are adolescents, and Xers see them as just that. Xers grew up taking care of their brothers and sisters when they were sixteen because both their parents had to work. There's a huge conflict in attitudes. What that looks like is frustration on the leadership side and a lack of investment in development in Second-Wavers. What Second-Wavers need is remediation to get them up to speed to become the adults and employees they need to be, but that's not typically what the Xer boss wants to invest in.

We may see massive amounts of turnover in industries as a result of this relationship. The companies that realize they need to spend more time with these incoming Second-Wavers are the ones that are going to grow. Setting up training and mentorship programs for Second-Wavers and spending the time and money to get them up to speed and be better communicators will pay off. An enlightened Xer realizes they get a better return on investment when they invest in their people and spend money on training because turnovers are expensive. I have many Millennials working for me. I know what they're interested in, how they respond, and what motivates them. The smart Xer is going to refocus and redouble their efforts on the training and development these Second-Wavers need.

Millennials: *"Friend Me"*

— • —

Millennials were born between 1982-2004. That's about 100 million people, making Millennials the largest generation in US history. They represent about 35% of the US population and about a third of the workforce. They are the most ethnically diverse generation in US history, which shouldn't be terribly surprising. If you take eighty-five-year-olds and older who live in the US and line them up, 5% are non-white. If you take five-year-olds who live in the US today and line them up, 52% are non-white. By 2045, the United States will be primarily a nonwhite country.

Millennials are the cutting edge of demographic history, and they're also the most educated generation in United States history. 39% of Millennials over the age of twenty-five have four-year college degrees. By contrast, in 1974, only 18% of Boomers over twenty-five had four-year college degrees. The third big trend we see in Millennials is that risk behaviors are the lowest on record. Cigarette use and alcohol consumption has plummeted since the early and mid '90s. They don't go out and drink for fun, like I used to when I was young. Also down are risk behaviors like not wearing seatbelts, drinking while driving, pregnancy, and abortion rates. There are some significant longitudinal trends taking place among Millennials.

This outcome is not at all surprising when taking into account their coming-of-age story. When I talk about the Millennials coming of age, the first thing I mention is the dramatic shift in parenting from the parents of Xer children to the parents of Millennial children. When it comes to hands-on parenting, it's like a faucet was turned on at some point in the mid-'80s and is still running today, flooding every aspect of society.

When Xers were young, the social economic conditions of youth were at an all-time low. Mortality rates were up, and parents, teachers, and policymakers—the whole community—rallied together to decide they needed to focus on their children and slow the downward spiral. Suddenly there were budgets allocated towards children and shows targeted towards children, every moment spent coddling and encouraging them. Parents were actually spending time with their kids, looking at their grades, helping them. We shouldn't be surprised Millennials are the way they are today.

Seven Traits of Millennials

1. Special—According to the Strauss-Howe theory, there are seven primary traits of Millennials. The first trait is special. Like Barney, their parents told them, "You are special." Today, older generations tend to consider Millennials as entitled. I don't think that's fair. The fact is, Millennials have been told they're special by parents, teachers, coaches, and the media all their lives. When they get to work and they're told, "Just do your job, dummy," it's a culture shock. In the workplace, Millennials want to feel they're an important part of a team, integral to the mission. It's not "me, me, me," it's about interaction.

2. Sheltered—They grew up in a time of rising protection by their parents; they didn't know anything else. There were always bicycle helmets, amber alerts, and different ways to buckle in a car seat. I didn't even have a car seat when I was growing up! Some people call Millennials the Snowflake Generation because this "sheltered" trait can be misconstrued for weakness, another unfair assumption. We can't blame a generation for the way they were raised, especially since they were raised by us, the very generation criticizing them.

3. Achieving—As I mentioned, Millennials have the highest graduation rate of any generation. They also have the highest AP scores. If you compare winning spelling bee words from decades past to the words of today, you'll see everything's been ratcheted up for Millennials.

1934 winning word: Brethren.

2004 winning word: Autochthonous.

People complain about kids today: they can't read, they can't write. The reality is, the material they're learning in high school right now is vastly more sophisticated than that of their parents and grandparents. In fact, *The American Journal of Psychology* did a report a couple of years ago stating the average IQ for a Millennial is seven points higher than their grandparents'.

4. Confident—Millennials' parents told them they're special, that they can achieve anything. I never had a conversation with my parents like that. They never said, "What do you want to do with your life? Where do you want to go? Let's work out a plan together." I was just sent out playing with my friends while my parents were working. Millennials draw their confidence from the sheer amount of attention their parents gave them. This confidence produces optimism, which was in short supply with Xers. We were cynical, sarcastic, and pessimistic, while Millennials were raised to feel confident they could accomplish anything.

5. Conventional—One of the things surveys show again and again is that all Millennials really want out of life is to be part of a community. They want to be good citizens. They want to be good parents. In fact, they actually want a lot of things their parents wanted. The parent/child generation gap is practically zero right now. Millennials buy the same clothes as their parents; they'll even listen to the same music and watch the same shows together. The original idea of the generation gap started with the Boomers: their parents wanted convention-ality, but Boomers wanted anything but conventionality. Millennials don't rebel that way, which is why they're going to be the ones to rebuild government because they actually believe institutions can make a difference. 9/11 had a huge impact on society, but for Millennials in grade school, the message was simple: there's a guy out there named Osama Bin Laden, and he's bad. The only way to get the guy is with the full force of the US military: all together as a team.

6. Pressured—This trait is especially prominent in Second-Wave Millennials. Interestingly, the suicide rate for young people is now higher than it's been in a very long time, and it's still going up. Millennials report more stress in their life than any other generation ever has. There's an immense level of pressure linked with the high achievement common in Millennials. They put a lot of pressure on themselves, as do their parents and society in general. Never before have private test scores been so visible to everyone else; it's everywhere, and (in the age of the internet) it's forever. Millennials are always thinking about how what they do today affects how they're going to be perceived tomorrow. They're careful about what they post on social media. The pressure they face forces them to think about the long-term.

7. Collaborative—Finally, Millennials are all about collaboration. They were raised with community service projects required for school and group projects common within the classroom. Then, of course, we saw the phenomenon called Facebook, and suddenly the internet was all about connecting, reaching out, and building community. Boomers and Xers have always been competitive in their life and work, but Millennials don't think that way. When I go into the workplace, I see Millennials working together on projects as if it's a given. In fact, they get mad if someone on their team is getting paid less than they are. A Millennial might approach the boss and say, "He does just as much as me; he should get paid what I'm paid." An Xer would never say that, but team values and collaboration are a big part of who Millennials are.

Combine these seven traits, and it makes for a very complex individual. Special, sheltered, achieving, confident, community-oriented, pressured, and collaborative. The oldest Millennial is thirty-six, but in ten years they're going to be the ones running things, the ones enacting the change our country so desperately needs. Understanding how to interact with them, how to work with them, and how to bring about the best results with them is going to be at the forefront of business and society for the next twenty years.

Millennials' Impact on the Future

In fifteen years, Millennials will be the dominant generation within the United States government, which has the potential to be amazing for our country. Much of the civic-mindedness and purposefulness of Millennials was instilled in them by their parents, who drove them to academic and social perfection. Now Millennials volunteer at the highest rate of any generation in US history. Of course, they're going to give 5% of their income to non-profits and, of course, they're going to work at a soup kitchen. It's just what they do.

Neil Howe and I did a survey in 2014 that asked this question: To what extent do you agree that helping others in need is a strong priority for you? You'd think that as you get older, you get more empathetic about people in need because you've encountered more of them. The reality is that Millennials scored higher than Xers and Boomers on that question. 83% of Millennials felt helping others was a strong priority, but only 69% of Boomers felt that way. Boomers are off finding themselves, and Millennials are out with their hands open, asking, "How can I help?"

We also asked, "To what extent do you agree it's important that a company you buy products from supports social causes?" Over 50% of Millennials said that's important to them. 46% of Xers said that and 48% of Boomers. Millennials are leading the charge. There's so much information available today about what food is made of. It used to be accepted that you simply didn't know where your food came from, and you didn't ask. You didn't want to know if that pig was slaughtered in distress or after a happy romp in the field. Amid all the transparency today, combined with the underlying philosophy of Millennials, we're witnessing a huge shift in consumerism.

But They're So Damn Sensitive!

Millennials are sensitive, but that's not a bad thing. I'm involved in a program called Allyship, conceived and run by a really impressive non-profit called Service Never Sleeps. The focus is on bridge-building by recognizing privilege and marginalization in today's society. While doing this work, it becomes crystal clear that Millennials are more sensitive than previous generations, more cognizant of their privilege. Millennials know there are three pronouns by which to address someone: him, her, and them. "Them" didn't even exist a couple of years ago. Millennials get the message way faster than Boomers and Xers: you can't build community unless you know your brothers and sisters who look different than you because a community is made up of all kinds of people and all kinds of ideas.

"Jennifer really needs to put a little more time into her reports," Dave the Boomer grumbles as he sifts through paperwork. "She half-asses this stuff." He glances at Samanthe, hoping she catches the hint that she too ought to put adequate time into her reports. But Samanthe frowns.

"I think she does her best," she offers.

"Ha. She cares more about doing it than doing it well."

Samanthe presses her lips together. He can try all he wants, but Dave won't make her talk poorly about Jennifer. Samanthe knows she has a family that she works hard to support. For Millennials like Samanthe, it's not all about me, me, me. Millennials are sensitive about everybody. In the workplace, this translates to the idea that if you want to motivate someone who works for you, you have to find out where they're coming from, what their story is. Stephen Covey is famous for saying, "First seek to understand in order to be understood."

This is interesting considering they were raised by Xers, whose view conflicts harshly with this one. But, in fact, it's because Xers were raised in the wild that they raised their kids in an opposite manner. Guess what's going to happen when Millennials become parents? They're going to reverse the trend and raise little free-range kids. It's the irony of generations: many traits are carried on, but some are reversed. Strauss and Howe predicted what Millennials would be like because they understood how Boomers and Xers were raised, and they knew Boomers and Xer parents would raise their kids in the opposite way. If you raise your child to be better than you were, then you're making the world a better place. If you can make your kid better than you, then you've achieved something.

Technology is a Part of Them

Let's get back to technology. These are Millennials we're talking about, after all, and the truth is, it always comes back to technology with Millennials. When it comes to First-Wavers, the technology they've invented and interacted with is a representation of who they are as a generation. Second-Wavers are more heavily influenced by technology than any other generation, and (at this point) we can't be sure if it's a positive or negative thing. The rapid rise in smartphones and the speed at which you can get information is very alluring to young people. Nowadays we see two-year-olds on iPads, tapping and swiping. How that story ends, we don't know.

Regardless of all that, there are a couple of big trends to notice when it comes to Millennials and technology. The amount of raw time a Millennial spends in front of a screen of any kind is eight hours a day. When they do that, they're not moving: they're static, focused on whatever's on the other side of that screen with a good amount of intensity. During this time, they tend to not be interacting with other people, although sometimes they are. That's a different kind of physical, mental, and emotional experience than any other generation in history has experienced. For the first time, young people are using IRL, which stands for "in real life"; they have to distinguish between real life and virtual life. Millennials blend the two seamlessly.

The alarmist's response to this would be, "Oh God, the entire cognitive process is going away." But we don't know what skills are going to be needed for the future. Maybe we'll need short attention spans, who knows? It's very difficult to know the type of skills and cognitive development that will be necessary in twenty or thirty years.

Millennials may seem less social than other generations, due in no small part to the fact that technology has enabled them to communicate without interacting in person. They're dependent on digital technology and inexperienced in face-to-face interaction because they're spending so much time in front of a screen. While technology is allowing them to explore new and exciting skills, it seems to be closing the door to other, age-old functions, like communication—an argument many bosses and managers make today, and one which I'll address.

They're Not Completely Unlike Us

In many ways, being a Millennial isn't easy. More so than other generations, Millennials are dealing with crushing levels of student debt. Forbes reported 57% of Millennials "regret how much they borrowed" for education, and now it's delaying their ability to buy a home, get married, and travel.

Of course, they've got a lot going for them too. For example, Millennials are fully embracing flexibility at work. While gig economy jobs may not be ideal in some ways, they do afford Millennials a significant amount of freedom. Millennials like the way being a fulltime freelancer or contractor gives them independence, career development, and learning opportunities a more traditional nine-to-five job simply wouldn't. Even within more traditional jobs, employers are embracing the notion of a more flexible work schedule. Half the US workforce has a job that's compatible with at least some teleworking, according to Global Workplace Analytics. Technology plays an important role in this dynamic. Thanks to near-ubiquitous Wi-Fi, the adoption of tablets, newer workplace communication tools like Asana and Slack, and the proliferation of co-working spaces, being productive outside the office is entirely possible.

While Millennials are used to processing a lot of digital information, they don't always prefer digital communication. Studies from the Pew Research Center show that although Millennials send more text messages than members of other generations, they also talk on their phone more than older adults think. And when they can't figure something out, they would rather talk to a person than get help online. "For many Millennials, person-to-person contact is still a reliable and effective solution to their problems—not something they fear or avoid," Nielsen Norman Group reported.

This applies in the workplace too. A Fortune/IBM study shows that when it comes to learning new professional skills, Millennials prefer face-to-face interaction and in-person coaching and mentoring. Additionally, although many people characterize Millennials as a generation of over-sharers, that same Fortune/IBM study revealed Millennials are more likely to draw a firm line between professionalism and personal sharing than older generations.

And it's not just Millennials who love technology. A Nielsen study found that older generations of adults are just as addicted to their mobile devices. Boomers are more likely to use technology during a family meal than their Millennial or Homelander counterparts. More than half of Boomers (52%) have admitted to using technology at the dinner table—12% more than Millennials and 14% more than Homelanders.

What Does This Mean for Managers?

First, don't assume Millennials are less communicative than other generations—but be aware that they usually communicate through different mediums. Millennials will appreciate employers and managers who have found flexibility in integrating communication technology in the workplace. Second, be open to Millennials' suggestions of new tools that can help them (and you) communicate. Finally, nothing will replace in-person communication. It's still key for all employees to have the opportunity for in-person meetings. For Millennials, in-person meetings are the best way to show you care about them.

Financial stress from student loans and job uncertainty means many Millennials are trying to save money on housing by moving back home with Mom and Dad. Some are using the money they save on rent to pay back student loans faster, so they can move on with their adult lives already. More than one-third of college seniors in 2016 planned to live at home for at least a year after graduation, according to the job website Indeed. Millennials grew up with parents who were highly involved in their children's emotional and educational development and activities. For employers looking to hire recent graduates, it's likely that prospective Millennial hires' parents are heavily involved in this process. That may mean answering questions from parents or even inviting parents into the office. Managers must be patient and understanding with parents.

Boomers led the way in their youth to be unconventional, antiestablishment, and countercultural. Xers followed Boomers' lead by being nonconforming, but in a different, more rule-avoiding way. Millennials, on the other hand, are a truly conventional generation in many respects. Gallup research revealed, "In addition to finding steady, engaging jobs, Millennials want to have high levels of wellbeing, which means more than being physically fit. Yes, Millennials want to be healthy, but they also want a purposeful life, active community and social ties, and financial stability."

Millennials are waiting longer than their parents and grandparents to get married, have children, and buy homes, but not because they don't want to follow the conventional path of owning a home and raising a family. They're delaying those things due to economic circumstances—student loans and tenuous employment situations. For employers, this means providing Millennials with predictable, stable opportunities to grow their skillset and a clear career path. Millennials don't like to "wing it." They would rather have a plan extending well into their future and know what to expect for their long-term development. Managers have to aptly explain benefits like health insurance and 401(k)s.

Dispelling the Myths

Older generations have many misconceptions about Millennials: They're lazy and perpetually late. Values like promptness and industriousness have gone by the wayside with them. Civilization as we know it is ending. But before you retreat to your fallout shelter, there is new research that proves otherwise. An increasing number of studies show Millennials are not slackers, and in fact may have an unhealthy dedication to hard work.

Millennials grew up in the Digital Age (after all), where everything is on and available all the time. They live in a twenty-four-hour news cycle where emails, texts, tweets, and memes are calling out to them at all hours from a device that is never more than an arm's length away—literally.

Part of the reason the "lazy" myth has been perpetuated is due to a different way of working that Millennials embrace. Used to doing things on the go, work may include answering emails from the gym or a coffeeshop. Millennials believe in working just as hard as everyone else, but they don't feel the need to be anchored to a desk and show face time at the office. They can work anywhere. While Millennials, like all of us, value time away from work, for many the workday does not have a traditional beginning and end. The nine-to-five schedule only exists in theory for Millennials.

Further, Millennials are more likely than older workers to forfeit earned time off, even though they typically earn the fewest vacation days. According to research by GFK for Project Time Off, American workers took just sixteen days of vacation per year in 2015—down from more than twenty days per year between 1978 and 2000.

They're No Strangers to Hard Work

Millennials are work martyrs. They are more likely than members of other generations to want to show complete dedication. They do not want to be seen as replaceable at work, and they want to stay in consideration for that next raise or promotion. First impressions and professional reputations are particularly important to them, according to research from Weber Shandwick. They believe the top way to build their reputation at work is by doing a good job and being prompt. Almost half of Millennials surveyed said volunteering for or accepting extra work is a good way to improve their professional reputation.

For those who work with Millennials, understanding their desire for flexible scheduling is critical to helping them succeed and feel professionally satisfied. The majority of Millennials "believe that flexible work schedules make the workplace more productive for people their age."

Without face time as an indicator of work, executives will have to adjust how they measure employee effectiveness. Millennials are keen on being given challenging but achievable goals, particularly if they come with proper support. Measuring their success, then, may include looking at their productivity, whether they are meeting goals and deadlines, how well they collaborate with coworkers, and the extent to which they contribute positively to the team or company. Millennials' desire for transparency and openness at work is a factor here as well. They want to work for companies where managers and executives are accessible and approachable, and are able to communicate effectively across platforms and follow up. Managers may want to start getting used to texting their employees.

Give Them the Roadmap

Xers are goal-oriented like Millennials, but they don't need a map because they're used to figuring stuff out on their own. Boomers definitely don't want a map; they're going to do it their own way through and through, no matter what you tell them. For Millennials though, if you give them a goal, they want a detailed, instructive roadmap showing them how to get to that goal. They want to know the exact steps they need to take to do it right the first time. Dave or Jennifer might say, "How come you need such handholding? Why do you need all that detail? I never get detail."

The reality is that Millennials have a different orientation around reaching goals. They've had more time and attention paid to them by their parents, teachers, coaches, everyone. Remember, Millennials don't like to fail, so they're going to want to check in all the time to ensure they're on the right track. They just want to do it right. They don't want to make mistakes; they're risk-averse. When you provide them a step-by-step plan, a clear roadmap, you're reducing the risk. Every step of the way they want the opportunity to check in with the manager to make sure each step was done correctly. Millennials' need for feedback comes from a place of habit; they're used to being checked in on frequently. This is even truer for Second-Wave Millennials than First-Wave Millennials.

They Strive for Perfection

In the same vein as their fear of failure, Millennials are constantly looking for the best way to do something. They want to achieve and, in the workplace, this can translate to high productivity. Millennials are going to search for more information, or find someone who has experience, or write and rewrite the presentation. For example, let's say a Millennial is in a manufacturing environment. If they're told they need to hang drywall, they want to know the very best way to hang it. What bonding element would be best to use? Where do they tape it to ensure the best possible results? They want instructions. Members of other generations who don't think that way view Millennials as stupid, incompetent, or needy. But they just want to do it right, so they can achieve the best results. Chances are, if you explain things, you'll be surprised by what they can do with the knowledge.

The responsibility for good communication is on the Boomer, not the Millennial: the boss, not the employee. The Boomer, because they're the boss, is the one who needs to figure out how to communicate effectively. That's the job of a manager. A lot of managers don't think about it that way, but the reality is, it's not up to the employees. Sure, employees need to fit into the culture and do their best, but it is up to the supervisor or manager to figure out the best way to communicate with the people who work for them. That involves understanding what makes a Millennial tick.

Hiring and Managing Millennials

——— • ———

Iconic Boomer Yoko Ono once said, "The thing that would improve my life is twenty-seven hours in a day. I could meet all my deadlines." As an Xer, I think I speak for my generation when I say that's a stupid idea. Generation X works within the time constraints of reality by developing their own structure, systems, and rules in a scrappy, purposeful way. Our rule is simple: there is no structure, so make it yourself, do perfect work, or lose your job.

Fast forward to the Millennial Generation—what's their deal with time management? They're not very good at it, and their managers are telling them, "There are no rules for time management—you need to figure it out on your own."

My unscientific, anecdotal observation is that Millennials are awesome. Generally speaking, they strongly want to do the right thing. They want to achieve their goals, they are committed to the company, and they don't want to let anyone down. In other words, their intentions are good.

If these chipper young professionals are so dedicated, why do they struggle with time management and meeting deadlines? Because their personalized parental helicopter dropped them off in a vast work ocean of unscheduled days. As children and young adults, their days were scheduled full of activities and events, with parents, coaches, and teachers telling them what to do and when. In an unintentional perversion of outcomes, the adults in their lives micromanaged them, but never taught these Millennials how to micromanage themselves. When they got to work, they were set adrift without helicopter Mom and Dad. As a manager, you need to pull off a rescue operation—get the Coast Guard and help these kids to solid ground.

Introduce Structure

There are simple things you can do in this regard. Introduce a structure for prioritizing tasks and projects. Have your Millennials organize their to-do list by "urgent," "high priority," and "low priority" based on their deadlines and the importance of the task. Also, help them see how they can break big projects down into smaller pieces. The feeling of accomplishment itself can spur Millennials to keep going. Breaking down large projects into their smaller component pieces can make tasks seem less overwhelming, help Millennials prioritize, and encourage them to keep moving forward. The positive feeling of crossing something off the to-do list feeds their need to achieve.

Gamification & Time Management Apps

As an Xer, your training took place on the street, with trial and error. Not for Millennials. It will help if they are taught in structured, classroom-like settings to be effective and productive with their time. Millennials are good students. They didn't skip classes like you did. If you schedule it, they will come.

Some workplaces have incorporated "gamification" into their workflow, rewarding employees for meeting incremental goals or deadlines and promoting teamwork to accomplish large projects on time. Many of these work gamification systems are available as mobile apps, allowing Millennials to be productive no matter where they work. For individual time management, Millennials may respond well to cross-platform apps. The app you recommend may depend on the challenge Millennials are facing. If they suddenly realize hours have passed and they don't know where the time went, try Rescue Time. As a training tool, the app will send weekly reports with feedback on what tasks are "stealing" time, and it provides accolades when the user makes improvements.

If they just need help focusing, Focus Booster is modeled on the Pomodoro method, with timers for "focus time" and "breaktime." For the environmentally-minded, the app Forest lets users plant a virtual tree and watch it grow the more productive the user is at work. The bottom line is, it's the manager's job to help with time management training, skills, and tools.

Crafting the Millennial Website

If you want Millennials on your team, you have to meet them where they are. To begin with, Millennials put a lot of value in first impressions. Millennials, particularly Second-Wave Millennials, are very adept at doing Google searches and finding websites that get them knowledge on your organization. They could size your entire company up in about a second and a half. If they look at your website and it doesn't seem inviting to them, they're not going to be interested in working for you. They want clarity about your mission and purpose. They want a website that doesn't have a lot of words. They want it simple and laid out in a user-friendly format. Like their Xer parents, they desire simplicity and efficiency.

Millennials are most likely to see your website on a mobile device, not a computer. Recently, I did an analysis of the number of people coming to our new company's website, and just a two-week analysis showed that 75% of eighteen to twenty-four-year-olds who checked the website saw it on a mobile device. You may have a nice-looking website on the computer, but if you don't craft it for mobile, that's a huge issue. You have to include the marketing and HR departments in building the website. You have to include input from managers about who you are and what you're like as a company. It sounds very tactical, just changing your website, but Millennials make decisions quickly, and these small things matter.

Ten years ago, employees didn't have the ability to peek into a company to figure out where they wanted to work. They just showed up and did a job interview. Now Second-Wave Millennials have x-ray vision when it comes to understanding what you're all about. You should put on the website what the larger purpose of the company is and why you exist. Remember, Second-Wave Millennials prioritize mission and purpose. It needs to be clear and clean. The internet and social media are windows into your company, and unless you understand what Millennials are interested in and meet them where they are, you're going to have a hard time attracting them.

Appealing to Their Sensibilities

To a Millennial, you're scary. Millennials are a nice generation. They're polite, caring, and pay attention to people's feelings. They invented Facebook, where you "like" people and make "friends." You, on the other hand, had murky MySpace. You had Pong, where your only advantage was reptilian speed, and later Atari, Space Invaders, and Pac Man, where you were constantly on the run from the bad guy. Every man for himself, right?

"Hey, get that presentation submitted already, will 'ya?" Dave the Boomer says roughly as he passes by Samanthe's desk. "Boss is waiting on it."

Samanthe flinches, hurt. "Sorry," she says, practically whispering. She can feel tears welling hot behind her eyes, and she fights them hard, determined not to cry. When Dave is out of sight, she whispers to Jennifer, "Hey, do you know if Dave is upset with me?"

Jennifer resists the urge to roll her eyes. She doesn't have the patience to mediate petty drama, nor does the company have time to waste on caring who's mad at who. She scoffs slightly, shaking her head. "Is this high school?"

Samanthe buries her chin in her chest, lost. For the rest of the day, she struggles to focus on her work, distracted and discouraged by her coworkers. Don't be mean to Millennials. Tough love does not work. Stay positive and point out their accomplishments.

Spend Time with Them

This may be the hardest thing for you to do, but you need to spend more time with your Millennials. Regular intervals of feedback are an essential element in managing Millennials. Your boss didn't spend much time with you, but you didn't want to be around him with his Boomer bad breath and stupid maxims about "early to bed, early to rise" anyway. Millennials actually trust and respect authority figures. It started with their parents, who were always supportive, caring, and flying the helicopter low and close to make sure they were safe from nearly every threat.

You don't need to spend long period of time with them, as your creepy boss did when he wanted to take you out for a drink after work. A short check-in every day for five minutes is perfect for Millennials. Their brains operate in short intervals anyway. For the time it takes to check their Facebook, load an Instagram of their adorably funny cat, and Snap a friend, you can cover the basics of their goals for the day and provide the tools for their success.

Ask three questions: What did you accomplish last week? What is your plan to accomplish this week? How can I help you get there? It makes a big difference in helping the Millennial understand that they're cared for and that you're paying attention to them, and it also keeps them on track in terms of their goals. Guided direction is crucial. You have to let them know you've got their back. Think of yourself as that teacher or coach you had when you were young who took a genuine interest in your growth and development. That is the kind of manager you need to be to your Millennials.

Reverse Mentoring

Though we may not want to believe it, the fact is we have a lot we can learn from Millennials at work. Xers and Boomers are increasingly serving as mentors to Millennials in the workplace, but the new trend is reverse mentoring, where Millennials provide guidance on new and innovative ways to approach the ever-changing demands of work. The benefits of traditional mentoring—where an older, more seasoned professional trains, teaches, and coaches younger employees— are well documented. Mentoring young employees helps them learn more about their jobs, their role in the company, their potential career trajectory, and how to advance professionally; it also gives older employees an increase in job satisfaction and purpose, builds their career legacy, and gives them a unique professional outlet.

While the benefits of traditional mentoring relationships are known, the benefits of reverse mentoring are less known. Reverse mentoring is the practice of matching older, seasoned professionals with younger employees, with a focus on having the Millennials mentor up. Millennials are loyal, team-oriented, innovative, and goal-focused. Using these traits, they often bring a new perspective to the workplace, with a desire to see the "greater good" in their job, their role in the company, and the company's role in the world. Giving Millennials the opportunity to convey that passion to older employees, who have been with the company a long time, can reenergize and reignite the dedication and enjoyment longtime employees and managers once had for their jobs.

This can lead to positive changes throughout all levels of the company, with an increase in experimentation, newly discovered efficiencies, and new business development opportunities. Reverse mentoring also gives seasoned professionals an opportunity to reflect on their own way of doing things and may widen their understanding of the way their organization and industry are changing. With reverse mentoring, older professionals have a unique opportunity to close their knowledge gap in areas like technology, social media, work-life balance, workplace trends, and more.

A long-term Sun Microsystems study of about 1,000 employees found that employees who participated in a mentoring program were 20% more likely to get a raise, and that went for both mentors and mentees. In addition, employees who received mentoring were promoted five times more often than those who did not have mentors.

For companies, setting up reverse mentoring is easy, as it can work within the structure of the company's ongoing, more traditional mentoring program. Cisco, for example, started their program by finding a champion within the organization to promote the program and set goals and metrics by which to measure success. Then the company focused on recruiting mentees (i.e. older employees) and then recruiting mentors—the younger employees who indicated interest in participating. The company also provided the mentors with resources, tips, ideas, and best practices for mentoring, as many had never been a mentor to someone in the past. Cisco's former business operations manager Laura Earle declared the reverse mentoring program a success, as it built relationships and helped all participants develop a better understanding of the company.

For a reverse mentoring relationship to work, many of the same rules apply as for a more traditional mentoring relationship. Both younger and older participants must keep an open mind and a positive attitude, trust each other, respect each other's viewpoints, and find ways to seek common ground. Both parties should set goals and commit to scheduling ongoing meetings to keep the relationship strong.

Be Specific

Often, when I'm speaking to managers of Millennial employees, I'm asked, "Why don't my Millennial employees follow directions?" As a manager, it can be frustrating to give an assignment only to find out a week later that the assignment is not completed. What's the deal? There are two things to know about Millennials that can help you with this ongoing management challenge: speed and specificity.

Since childhood, Millennials have been conditioned to receive guidance and feedback at a high degree of frequency. Instant feedback on their computer-based quizzes and tests, Google searches, texting, and Snapchatting with friends has all had a profound influence on the expectations of speedy response times. Particularly in school, Millennials were tested, evaluated, graded, and given feedback more often than any other generation to date. Older generations indulged in the virtue of patience simply because things took longer to happen back then. Older generations understand waiting. But Millennials were not raised in an environment where waiting was normal. Instant feedback on almost everything is the norm.

As a manager in the workplace, consider checking in with your Millennial employees a few times a day about the assignment you've provided. You might think that's overkill, but to a Millennial, it's normal. Frequent check-ins allow you to assess their ability to stay on task and make sure they understand how to proceed. Also, provide directions to Millennials with a high level of specificity. They are fairly dependent on you as a manager. They want specific directions on how to do an assignment correctly and also an explanation of why it is important. Millennials were raised in a highly planned and structured environment. Free time and play was not something Millennials did—everything was planned for them. Another contributing factor in their need for specificity is that they hate to take risks and hate to fail. An open-ended assignment for them is viewed as a risk. Be assured that if there is a YouTube video on how to do something, they're watching it.

A LifeCourse Associates survey revealed, "69% of Millennials say they like their supervisor to provide them with 'hands-on guidance and direction.' Only about 40% of Boomers and older Xers said the same." In response, many companies are doing away with the annual performance review; it's being replaced with more frequent meetings, updates, goal tracking, and evaluations with more specificity. As a manager, it's important to provide instructions that have clear goals and a definitive process that assures them they're going in the right direction. Providing frequent cycles of open and honest feedback will have positive effects—increased loyalty, professional satisfaction, and more employee engagement. Millennials will feel valued, cared for, and motivated to meet their goals. Incorporating these two simple elements—speed and specificity—means they'll be more likely to stay with the company for the long run, ultimately reducing recruitment and retention costs.

What They Like in the Workplace

Let me tell you something Millennials don't need in the workplace: an open, modern office with windows, lounges, ping-pong tables, a smoothie bar, and nap rooms. Thanks to images of excess from some of Silicon Valley's tech startups, a lot of executives come to me worried about their office environment. Will their lack of budget (or space) for a ping-pong table put them at a disadvantage when it comes to hiring the best and brightest Millennials?

I tell hiring managers that while "perks" similar to those offered by giants like Google and well-funded startups may attract Millennials, those cool office features don't keep Millennials fulfilled in the long run. Hiring is a serious expense and commitment, and if you want the best Millennials to stay with your company for more than a year, there are other things you should do.

Setting incremental deadlines and targets, and communicating how their project and role fit into the company's mission, will help Millennials see their path forward. Overall, they aren't looking for the coolest open concept office or best smoothies at work. They do want an open communication culture and the best opportunities for professional growth. Flexibility with work-life balance will help too. The companies that are able to show those perks are the ones that will attract the best Millennial employees and keep them around for the long haul.

Trust

Trust is one of the keys to helping Millennials feel professionally valued in the workplace. Allowing them to manage their own schedules and providing work-life balance assistance through telework or flexible hours shows Millennials they are trusted. Although new Millennial employees may need guidance and limits on telework and flex scheduling to ensure the team is supported, Millennials like working for companies that don't chain them to desks when they can work just as productively elsewhere.

In-Person Engagement

One trend I've been noticing in workplaces is an empty breakroom, where employees would typically gather to take a break from their work routine. There is a generational explanation for this, and it is not that people are necessarily working harder. The fact is that younger employees are more likely to take breaks at their desk, checking social media on their mobile device or listening to podcasts. Remember, Millennials are digital natives. In school and at home, they've always had more electronic devices and on-demand media than Boomers ever dreamed possible. With computers in the classroom and at home, the growing ubiquity of smartphones, Wi-Fi everywhere, and video on-demand, it's no surprise that the generation that grew up with technology is very comfortable engaging with it. In addition, the ability to work from anywhere for many Millennials has made engaging with people in the physical office less critical to productivity.

In recent years, some companies have tried to rein this in and force more in-person engagement among employees. Notably, IBM in 2017 brought back into the office the company's work-at-home employees, terminating most telecommuting options as a way to encourage more collaborative product development, comradery, and even company loyalty.

Forcing employees to come into the office is, in part, an overblown response to an ongoing myth about Millennials: that they prefer to avoid in-person conversations with others, opting for text instead of talk. In fact, repeated studies have shown Millennials do like in-person communication and recognize its importance in their career and professional development.

While some new employees may retreat to their mobile devices until they develop professional friendships, Millennials do come out of their shells. In particular, they seem to prefer it to digital communication when they need to get help with a project or task, when it comes to learning career-place skills and processes, and in coaching and mentoring relationships. For managers of Millennials, there are a number of ways to encourage in-person communication. First, have an open-door policy with both the physical space and with communication styles. Regularly hosting "office hours" (the way Millennials' college professors did) can encourage Millennial employees to walk into executives' offices and chat about the workplace and their goals and strategies.

Create opportunities for teamwork, such as professionally-related volunteer opportunities, in-person trainings, and activities. Millennials are more emotionally connected to jobs in which they understand and have an active role in how their company contributes to the "greater good" in the community and the world.

And there's always food. Over the summer, I had a meeting at Bloomberg's headquarters in New York. On the sixth floor was a massive reception area with a smorgasbord of free snacks and Millennials buzzing around everywhere. Coming out of college, many Millennials are comfortable with food-oriented activities. Few things get people away from their desks like treats in the breakroom—but managers may want to center a meeting or activity around those treats to prevent the treats being taken straight back to Millennials' desks.

Getting Them to Take Their Work Seriously

A common question that comes up when I'm training executives who work with Millennials is, "How can I get my Millennial employees to take their work seriously?"

But the idea that Millennials don't take their work as seriously as their older professional counterparts is another myth. Studies have shown that in many ways, Millennials are workaholics. Almost half (48%) of Millennials "think it is a good thing to be seen as a work martyr by the boss," a higher percentage than any other generation surveyed, according to a research by Project: Time Off. The difference in the way Millennials work is often the cause of the misconception that they aren't taking work seriously. Technology allows many people to work anytime, from anywhere. For some employees, that means they need to spend less time at their desk in the office. Social media and online project management systems, email and mobile devices, and remote desktops let Millennials stay connected to work wherever they are.

If Millennials in a workplace don't seem to be taking their work seriously, managers are often able to correct the situation through effective communication, goal-setting, and mentoring.

They're most engaged in their work when the key factors we've discussed are firmly in place. If you are convinced that your Millennial employee is not taking their job seriously, start a dialogue where he or she does most of the talking and you do most of the listening. Make your case—put all the cards on the table and do your best to listen. Sometimes it's hard to get to the root cause of the issue, especially if your relationship is strained or frustrating. Not all hires are a guarantee fit for the role, but if this is happening with more than one employee, you might need some coaching of your own.

Here Come the Parennials!

Now First-Wave Millennials—born in the 1980s and early 1990s—are becoming parents and, like all generations, they are putting their own mark on raising children. In this age of generational label overkill, they've even been given their own name: Parennials. As these Parennials transition to adulthood, they bring with them a brand-new style of parenting that reflects their priorities in work/life balance that will affect employers for the next couple of decades.

And there are lots of them—already, more than sixteen million Millennial women have children, and the number is growing by one million a year. Because they're having children later in life than previous generations, when their career is more established, they may have a better idea of what they want in life and in work. If you are an employer of these Parennials, you will want to readjust your programs and resources to reflect their needs as new parents. Here are a few ways employers can do that:

1. Work to keep childcare stress at bay.
An increasing number of workplaces are offering onsite policies that are childcare-friendly. If onsite daycare isn't possible, offering pre-tax childcare savings or flex spending accounts (FSAs) and financial counseling as parents adjust to the reality of new expenses can help increase corporate loyalty among Parennials.

2. Set parent-friendly policies and schedules.
Harvard Business Review reported, "Some organizations have implemented a policy that no meetings will start prior to 9:30 a.m. or end later than 4:30 p.m. This simple move cuts down on the anxiety surrounding timely daycare pickup and drop-off, and the expense related to daycare overtime charges. When parents aren't worried about running late, they can keep their mental energies focused on the business."

In addition, offering perks such as closing the office early on Halloween, offering job shares (two people work twenty hours per week each), or providing paid time off for parent-teacher conferences and school functions can go a long way.

3. Invest more in telecommuting and remote communications.

Flexibility around how, when, and where work is done can all help keep Parennials engaged and productive. Some companies have found that investing in teleconferencing technology can help allow for schedule and work location flexibility while keeping coworkers connected and engaged in the workplace.

Some Millennial and Generation X entrepreneurs are responding to these specific flexibility needs by creating professional co-working spaces attached to daycare centers or playrooms, such as "Play, Work, or Dash" in Northern Virginia.

4. Set up workplace parent support groups.

A new take on mentoring programs at work are parenting support groups. Millennials are the first generation who can get so much parenting advice online, but using the shared interest in parenting and how to juggle work and life can build bonds between coworkers and present new opportunities for mentorship. Millennials are giving birth to five of every six babies today, so (as an employer) consider building programs and allocating resources now to help keep (and attract) the best Millennial employees.

The Rise of Pink-Collar Jobs

Hourly work has changed significantly in the past two decades, with many blue-collar jobs (particularly in manufacturing and construction) declining in number. But so-called "pink-collar" hourly jobs have been soaring, with employment in educational services, healthcare, and social assistance increasing substantially. In fact, a recent Bureau of Labor Statistics report showed four of every ten jobs that the United States economy added in December 2016 were in healthcare or social assistance. The boom is expected to last for at least another decade. Even with the positive job growth, pink-collar industries face demographic headwinds, and hiring managers in these fields need to be ahead of the issues to attract and retain top Millennial employees. In these fast-growing industries, it can be difficult to find enough qualified workers to fill jobs.

Pink-collar jobs tend to skew heavily female, particularly in healthcare and education. The ratio of women to men in healthcare fields such as home health aides, medical assistance, and registered nurses is nine to one, according to the US Bureau of Labor Statistics. Many men feel unsuited for pink-collar work or are simply uninterested in working in a field so dominated by women, leaving hiring managers with a smaller potential workforce.

Hiring managers in pink-collar industries are thus facing a two-pronged challenge: find, attract, and retain the smartest and hardest-working Millennials, and overcome the stigma some men feel against these fields. Hiring managers can take specific actions to help overcome these challenges. The first step to effectively recruit Millennials is to understand what makes them different from older generations. In recruiting messages, highlight the growth and long-term career potential in your industry. It's not a difficult story to tell: the numbers will speak for themselves. However, make sure you translate those raw numbers into how a job in the industry can develop into a career with opportunities for advancement, long-term professional satisfaction, and work/life balance—the things beyond job security that Millennials are seeking.

Hiring managers should also emphasize how their participation in these pink-collar industries will make a positive difference in society and their own communities. Millennials desire to be part of something bigger than themselves, so tying their work to a larger mission goes a long way in attracting Millennials. Finally, Millennials get impatient easily, especially when dealing with outdated technology during the application process. Make sure your application process is clear, simple, and speedy. If it's not, the best and brightest will see that as a sign your company doesn't appreciate the value of technology that can streamline their work environment once they're there.

The demand for pink-collar jobs is growing and is likely to keep growing over the next decade. At the same time, demographic trends suggest that the supply of able-bodied workers is decreasing. Combine this with the stigma of pink-collar work, and you have a challenging equation for employers. Employers that will come out on top are those who value Millennials and adjust their hiring and career advancement practices accordingly to attract the best and brightest of this generation.

The Decline of Millennials in Blue-Collar Industries

Unfortunately for the current leaders in blue-collar industries, Millennials—the very workers who in the years to come will be needed to replace outgoing blue-collar retirees—have shown little interest in blue-collar work. For example, there is a declining percentage of twenty-five to thirty-four-year-old workers in construction (6.9% in 2015, down from 7.9% in 2000). According to a 2013 Georgetown University study, 35% of eighteen to twenty-four-year-olds worked in a blue-collar jobs in 1980. By 2010, that share had dropped to 19% as the population of people that age in the United States grew.

Why is this happening? In addition to lower demand in some sectors, like manufacturing, blue-collar work has acquired a stigma that drives away Millennials, including stagnant or low wages and a lower quality of life. Millennials choosing hourly jobs are often seeking out ones that don't necessarily require continuing education or apprenticeship-like training, such as sales.

Tips for Hiring Millennials in Blue-Collar Fields

How can managers in these blue-collar fields ensure they're sending positive messages to potential Millennial employees? There are specific, actionable strategies you can use to attract and retain Millennials. In addition to the techniques we've discussed, hiring managers must make dedicated efforts in the hiring process to highlight the long-term career potential and growth in these fields. Counter negative assumptions and stereotypes with success stories and early, positive associations. For example, RV manufacturer Thor Industries offers tours to eighth graders and their parents and also has a presence in schools that lets both audiences know about the well-paid, stable work environment the company provides. The marketing campaign Go Build Alabama, that highlighted above-average earning potential for skilled laborers and emphasized construction as an accessible field to people without college degrees, helped boost applications to apprenticeship programs in the state by 73%. Other states have started replicating the program.

Hiring managers should also promote teamwork and leverage Millennials' team-oriented attitudes. This means recruiting friend groups and creating immersive, multiday orientation programs that allow time for new hires to bond with their new coworkers. Allow connections during the workday through social media and text messaging without assuming these tools are hurting productivity; they can be incorporated into the ways Millennials are used to working.

Managers and executives should also leave the door open for new hires to contribute their ideas. In industries where there may not be much room for this type of input, make it clear how the work Millennials are doing is integral to the team's mission. Don't be shy about expressing appreciation for their ideas. In addition, emphasize how the work they're doing helps the larger world or offer volunteer opportunities to increase professional engagement and fulfillment. While hiring managers of hourly workers in blue-collar industries say the jobs can offer a steppingstone to a fruitful career, it's up to those same managers to convince young job-seekers of this, which requires a new approach to hiring and coaching Millennials.

Busting the Millennial Job-Hopping Myth

It's said that employee loyalty is dead. After all, it used to be that you joined a company and stayed there until you retired and received your gold watch. Thirty years ago, when you joined General Electric or IBM, you would stay for twenty years. Now I hear bosses say, "There's no loyalty these days. If something better comes along, my employees will pack up and move on." Well, guess what? They're right, there is no loyalty—the employer has no loyalty to his employees.

The average length of time people work for companies has dropped over the years, and while the assumption is that the employee is responsible for this trend, it's actually the companies that are driving this trend. Companies are not as stable as they used to be; they shift their strategy more often in the hypercompetitive environment, and the amount of incentives they offer has gone down considerably. In other words, companies no longer give employees a reason not to quit. Companies come and go at the speed of light, and defined benefit plans are a thing of the past. Furthermore, companies may not offer opportunities to develop employees' skillsets. So why stay?

Boomer and Xer bosses think Millennials job-hop a lot. Well, they do. Everybody who's young job-hops. That just happens at that age. In fact, the Bureau of Labor Statistics reported that Xers actually job-hopped more than Millennials when they were their age. Boomers were not job-hoppers, but again, that's because companies were more loyal to them and they, in turn, were more loyal to companies.

Many research reports recently cite that the number one reason Millennials leave their job is they don't feel they're being developed and learning the skills they need for their future. If companies focus on the needs of their employees and manage them better, they'll keep them longer. Turnover is expensive, so the company will save a lot of money if they can keep employees for ten years, as opposed to having ten different employees over a ten-year period. Most companies know deep in their bones they need to spend more time and money developing their employees, yet by the time the budget for the year is put together, training and development don't make the cut. Millennials want to gain the skills they need to move up in the company and in the world, and it's your responsibility to provide that.

To the extent that they do hop around, it's more about young employees' search for their professional strengths, interests, and career paths, according to a study by the Bureau of Labor Statistics. If you want your best Millennial employees to stick around, you need to understand that for Millennials, loyalty is a two-way street. If an employer is not investing in their professional development and satisfaction, there's a good chance they'll hit the road. Wouldn't you? According to a survey done by Deloitte earlier this year, 44% of Millennials say, if given the choice, they would like to leave their current employers in the next two years, particularly if "there is a perceived lack of leadership-skill development." More than six in ten Millennials (63%) say their "leadership skills are not being fully developed" at work. Fortunately, as an employer, you can do things to ensure Millennial loyalty.

Companies should capitalize on aligning company values to the personal values of their top Millennial employees. More than 80% of Millennials who plan to stay with their company for at least another five years believe their personal values are shared by the organizations they work for, according to Deloitte. This is a strong indication that Millennials choose to work for and stay with employers whose values reflect their own.

Millennials prioritize purpose over growth or profit maximization, which is one of the reasons the top three fields for Millennials are education, environment, and healthcare. Broadly speaking, Millennials' personal goals are traditional. They seek a good work/life balance, want to own their own homes, and strive for financial security that allows them to save enough money for a comfortable retirement. The ambition to make positive contributions to their organizations' success and/or to the world in general also rate highly. As an employer, assisting Millennial employees in reaching some of these goals can help engender loyalty.

The companies successfully keeping turnover down and instilling a long-lasting sense of loyalty in their Millennial employees seem to have common themes:

- **Identifying, understanding, and aligning with Millennials' values**

- **Supporting Millennials' ambitions and professional development**

- **Having a mentor**

A Deloitte survey shows that loyalty to an employer is driven by understanding and support of Millennials' career and life ambitions, as well as providing opportunities to progress and become leaders. Having a mentor is incredibly powerful in this regard. Those intending to stay with their organization for more than five years are twice as likely to have a mentor (68%) than not (32%).

However, like all generations, pay and financial benefits drive Millennials' choice of organization more than anything else. "But when salary or other financial benefits are removed from the equation, work/life balance and opportunities to progress or take on leadership roles stand out. Those factors are followed by flexible working arrangements, deriving a sense of meaning, and training programs that support professional development. An employer that can offer these is likely to be more successful than its rivals in securing the talents of the Millennial Generation."

Every incoming generation changes the shape of a workplace. Boomers brought long hours and an almost devotional approach to work. Xers brought work-life balance. Now Millennials are leaving their own footprint: a flexible, purpose-driven workplace with plenty of professional development opportunities.

They Think Your Company is Boring. How Can You Change Their Minds?

The insurance industry is boring. At least, that's the way Millennials see it. Research by The Institutes, an insurance non-profit, a few years ago revealed that "boring" was the number-one word Millennials associated with insurance. Those experienced in the industry know that's not true, but how does the insurance industry break this misperception?

And how can agents and brokers change it to capture the new, powerful workforce flowing into the ranks?

In many ways, Millennials want from their jobs the same things as previous generations, but they have different priorities and expectations of their workplace and require different best practices to be happy and fulfilled in their career. Insurance agents and brokers should consider rethinking their activities to meet these priorities and expectations. These are the building blocks to attract and retain the best and brightest Millennials:

1. The first area is **getting Millennials' attention.** Doing so will take a coordinated combination of a strong digital presence and a personalized approach to recruiting. This includes a website that is clean, uncluttered, shows the insurance company's connection to the demands of digital media, and showcases the company's mission and value proposition. As digital natives, Millennials' first impression of a company often comes digitally. This may mean going beyond a company's website and honing in on career-focused online presences such as Glassdoor or social media platforms, in addition to being responsive and approachable both online and off. According to the Deloitte Insurance Outlook 2017, technological innovation will be key to meeting challenges in the coming years.

2. Fortunately, digital tools can help with the second area of focus: **creating and promoting a company climate that is positive and team-oriented.** Millennials prefer teamwork over competition and gravitate toward conscientious employers who try to make a positive difference. They will also be

more loyal to companies that foster their career development, help them achieve their professional goals, and publicly value their contributions. Once your insurance organization has recruited and hired these top-tier Millennials, manage them on a day-to-day basis with close but nurturing supervision, mentoring, and coaching.

3. If Millennials had their way, the "annual performance review" would go the way of the fax machine. Millennials grew up with "Google" as a verb, as in "to google" virtually any answer to any question. More recently, services like Apple's Siri, Amazon's Alexa, and other digital concierges make finding information even more effortless. Ever since they were young, they were tested and graded at an alarming frequency. Millennials are uniquely conditioned to expect speed and frequency, especially as it relates to their performance goals. The dreaded annual performance review, which was never very popular, is fast becoming an antiquated relic.

Providing frequent and tight cycles of honest and open feedback will more than pay off in productivity and employee engagement. Engaged employees feel valued and have more professional satisfaction, tend to be more motivated, more likely to meet their goals, and more likely to stay with a company in the future. Some of the top-rated companies and best places to work have all but ditched the traditional, top-down annual performance evaluation in favor of more frequent, 360-degree reviews. These includes GE, Adobe, and Deloitte.

Top Four Reasons Millennials Quit Their Jobs

The top four reasons Millennials leave their jobs might be less about Millennials and more about their managers. When I worked at Gallup, our consulting mantra revolved around the notion that your manager is responsible for 85% of your experience with the company you work for; they can make or break you. The reason for high Millennial turnover is simple: bad management. Listed below are four reasons Millennials say they are leaving their job, and each of these reasons has to do with the difference between good management practices and bad management practices:

1. "No one is asking for my feedback." If your Millennial isn't happy, find out why. This is Management 101. Frequent check-ins are critical, especially early in one's career and especially for Millennials.

2. "I wasn't clear on opportunities for advancement." Provide clear opportunities for advancement (in excruciating detail).

3. "The job was advertised as one thing, but it turned out to be something else." Never inflate or misrepresent a role. Be completely honest about job expectations. Recruiters in HR try to put their best foot forward, but sometimes if the job seems too good to be true, it is. Always temper job expectations with reality about the job.

4. "It seemed like no one cared about me." This is a big one. Remember, Millennials grew up with an entire team looking out for their wellbeing.

Transitioning into the workplace can be an entirely different environment than their life experience ' up until their first job.

They Dig Corporate Social Responsibility

A 2011 Deloitte survey found Millennials who participated frequently in company-sponsored volunteer work are far more likely than their nonvolunteering peers to rate their corporate culture as positive, to be proud to work for their company, to feel loyal, to recommend their company to a friend, and to be very satisfied with their employer and with the progression of their career. Millennials are dedicated to corporate social responsibility, and not recognizing this dynamic can lead to Millennial disengagement and may even prompt them to challenge their employer on issues where they disagree.

Employers need a way to scratch that Millennial itch. Make sure your social responsibility programs are not just ad-hoc afterthoughts, but are integrated into the company's core strategy and purpose. Allow Millennials to do social responsibility work on company time. This is worth the investment, as they will be much more likely to work longer hours on the project you need them to do. Not only can you attract and retain the most talented Millennials, but you will build a bond of trust that will pay big dividends in the future.

Be Transparent

Remember Edward Snowden? At twenty-seven, he was the source of a series of leaked documents from the National

Security Agency. He disclosed classified secrets in order to expose the "surveillance state" of the US government. In his role as an analyst for the NSA, Snowden had access to classified material on a government program named PRISM that gave the government nearly unlimited access to every US citizens' emails and web-browsing activity. Snowden, a Millennial, was well-aware of the risks he was taking in exposing this top-secret program. Is it just a coincidence he's a Millennial? Not a chance. What do his actions tell us about Millennials in the workplace, and what do employers need to know about managing this new generation?

Technology is a Millennial's best friend. According to a recent survey by generations consultancy LifeCourse Associates, 93% of Millennials use social media for personal reasons, compared to 80% of Xers and 61% of Boomers. As long as technology is Millennials' best friend, there is an expectation that this friend or those responsible for the technology will not betray them. When Sergey Brin and Larry Page started Google (both Xers), they came up with a company slogan they still use today: "Don't Be Evil." Little did they know, they created an expectation for an entire generation.

Millennials trust technology, in part because technology has been an enabling partner from an early age—a source of entertainment, a way to stay close with friends and share things with them, even a way to help with schoolwork. Their parents, whom they also trust, gave them their first smartphone in order to stay in touch. Technology is not just a lifeline for Millennials, it is their life. Millennials don't mind that you may be watching them, but they do mind if you are doing it secretly. Companies should be clear about their privacy laws, and they should be upfront that, yes, they do have the ability to access employees' emails, but they are not evil; they only do it for good reasons.

When Boomers were young, their biggest fear was oversight from Big Brother. George Orwell's *1984* (written in 1949) was the guidebook for civic distrust of large institutions. Protecting privacy, particularly from the subversive forces of a centrally-controlled government or institution, resonated with an entire generation. Millennials, on the other hand, gladly put cameras in their own rooms and post the most intimate details of their daily activities for all to see.

Yes, they will share almost anything, but they have an expectation that everyone else is sharing as well. The Millennial quid pro quo is, "I'll be transparent, but I expect that you will be transparent too," even in the case of the US government, large institutions, or their employer. Millennials routinely share information about their salaries with coworkers and friends. When there's a perception that an institution is being nothing short of 100% transparent, Millennials will often push back.

According to Pew, 60% of Millennials think Snowden's release of NSA classified data serves the public interest, while just 46% of older generations believe this. Among those over sixty-five years old, only 36% are in agreement. The IRS scandal and now the NSA leaks have been a wakeup call for Millennials that our leaders (especially those over fifty)—whether Republicans or Democrats—are all the same when it comes to sequestering information intended for the public.

It is important to realize that when it comes to Millennials, their formative years with technology are something us older folks have never experienced. And this experience has shaped their attitudes—probably permanently. In other words, this is an attitude that they will not grow out of. This is not a "young person thing." This is for keeps.

For them, technology has always been free and transparent. Millennials don't like double standards. There is no expectation of privacy, but there is an expectation of transparency. If you're in HR, I recommend arranging some professionally-facilitated focus groups around this topic with your Millennial population. Find out what's on their minds. It's better to hit off a potential problem before you get whacked like the US government did. And don't expect the whacking to stop anytime soon. This is the tip of the iceberg.

Most employers will do good to go out of their way to be as transparent as possible about the decisions they make. Reevaluate what you disclose to employees and consider loosening the reins on information that does not entirely compromise your company's mission. And, if there is information you can't share, be explicit about why. For Millennials, honesty will trump secrecy all day long.

Millennials have told me they don't like where they work because their CEO says one thing and does another. A CEO might *say*, "Our people are the most important asset here. We work as teams. We're collaborative." But none of that is *actually* happening in the company. Millennials expect authentic leadership. If you're not going to be people-first, it's okay, but you have to be honest about it. Millennials have big bullshit meters. They can spot it from a mile away.

Set Millennials Free

Another important piece of advice that often goes overlooked when it comes to Millennials in the workplace: on a long weekend, set your Millennials free! Just because you as a Boomer or Xer grew up in a "work is life" culture does not mean Millennials feel the same way. In the Boomer world of work, it was in early, out late. Boomer adults took work seriously, some would say too seriously. They shattered the nine-to-five paradigm and put meaning to the term "workaholic."

In the 1990s, Generation X redefined the work environment once again with a pay-for-performance mentality. For an Xer, it didn't matter how long you worked, it just mattered that the job got done. These techno-literates used their creativity and adaptability to find new ways to solve problems and still find time for work/life balance. Now here come the Millennials, and once again, they will be redefining the work environment (but probably not until over 50% of them are over thirty in the 2020s, replacing Xers in management positions). In the meantime, be clear about goals, check in frequently on their progress (be positive and constructive), and give them the tools they need, but don't make them stick around on a Friday if they can manage to finish the work on Thursday.

———— • ————

Samanthe is typing at her desk when her boss, Zach, strides into the office. Early-thirties, dark hair, and donning a trimmed beard, he looks every part the First-Waver he so unabashedly is. "Hey, guys," he calls out. "Quick update: from now on, we're going to do most of our work communication through Slack. Cool?"

Samanthe's face lights up. Josh leans back in his chair and nods happily. Jennifer shrugs. Across the room, Dave looks up in bewilderment. "*Slack?* What the heck is that?"

Zach grins. "Cloud-based work collaboration platform. It's easy. You'll get used to it."

Frowning, Dave shakes his head. "*Cloud*-based ... Jeeze, I have no idea how to do this computer stuff. I'm really out of my depth here."

"It's okay," Samanthe reassures him with a bright smile. "I'll teach you." Glancing at Zach, "Is the program up?"

Zach nods. "Yep. You should all have the invite in your email by now. Go ahead and get started, and we'll go from there. Thanks!"

With that, he disappears back to his office.

"Man," Dave grumbles, "I think I made a big mistake coming here. You mean to tell me from now on we're going to do all of our work through some internet program? Good lord, George Orwell must be turning over in his grave right about now." He stands up. "I'll go have a word with the boss." But Samanthe's already at his desk, typing on his computer. "Hey, what do you think—"

"Oh, take a seat, ol' man," she says. "I'm going to teach you this, and you're gonna like it. Okay?"

Dave raises an eyebrow. "But—"

"Nope. No buts. We're doing this." She gets back to work,

opening Slack. Jennifer chuckles and shakes her head. Josh flashes Sam a thumbs-up. Dave groans, taking his seat while Sam creates his username and password. She writes it down on a slip of sticky paper. Then she logs him into the company Slack forum.

Dave watches intently. "I guess that doesn't look so bad," he admits.

"Pretty self-explanatory. These are your threads. Here are your channels, where you'll spend most of your time communicating with the team for our various tasks. For instance, PR and marketing will each be their own channel, as will sales. Each task will have its own channel, where we can all discuss what needs to be done and follow and evaluate our productivity."

Dave nods his head thoughtfully. He likes that word. Productivity.

"Lastly," Samanthe says, "here are your direct messages. This is how you talk to Zach, me, Josh, Jen, and whoever else you need to speak with about work."

"But what about the conference room?"

Samanthe smiles knowingly. "Dave, how many chairs are in that room?"

He shrugs. "How should I know?"

"Guess."

He pinches his chin, remembering. "A dozen?"

"Thereabouts. Now, how many employees in our division?"

"Thirty."

"Right. Obviously we can't fit thirty people into a conference room with only twelve chairs. But I kind of figured we wouldn't be using that space anyway. I guess it's more of an on-boarding area for new recruits, like us. With Slack, we don't have to get up out of our chairs every time we need to hold a team meeting. You don't have to walk all the way to Zach's office whenever you need to ask him a question. Heck, he might be on an important phone call, in which case you've wasted those few minutes trying to get ahold of him. Instead, just check out his avatar here. If he's 'away,' he might be busy, but you can send him a message anyway, and he'll see it as he logs on. If he's there, his avatar will have a green dot that says 'available.' This will definitely jumpstart our productivity."

Dave hears that word again, and he likes it. And again, he gapes openly at Samanthe, like she is some foreign specimen. Only this time, his face is marked with pride. "Jeeze, kid. I'm impressed."

Samanthe takes a bow. "Why, thank you, sir."

Dave chuckles. "Okay … well, I'll give it a try. But if I run into any issues, can I ask you for help?"

"Of course!" she says.

"Thanks, Samanthe."

"Welcome," she says nonchalantly, already on her way back to her desk, where she logs onto Slack and starts creating several different channels her coworkers forgot about. By the end of the day, she'll have become the most active team member on Slack, and her own productivity will have skyrocketed. And Dave will admit a begrudging respect both for the young spritely coworker across the room and for this new and exciting program.

By all accounts, the new recruits are starting to get along.

Millennial Lifestyle Themes

——— • ———

Millennials are a social generation. They're connected to their friends, their parents, and the community they live in. They have a positive and optimistic relationship with authority figures. They embrace people who are unlike them. If Millennials are positive, community-oriented, and social, what does that mean for the future? The answer is already beginning to play out in something called the "sharing economy." Examples of this include Uber and Airbnb. It's a participatory economy, connecting people to businesses in a digital way.

When you call an Uber, you get into a complete stranger's car. From a Boomer or an Xer's perspective, that's strange, inappropriate, and just plain dangerous. They don't trust this new system. Previous generations created these walls between people and commerce that prevented things like Uber from existing, but Millennials are tearing down all those walls. They've created a community of trust.

James Surowiecki wrote a book called *The Wisdom of Crowds*. In it he talks about the value of participatory democracy, and he sets a theoretical framework where societies come to better decisions when everybody has input, as opposed to just an elected few. If everybody has a vote about the way things go, we'll reach better outcomes. There's trust involved in the whole of the people, and that's a very Millennial concept. It's what I call "positive prosocial." The whole sharing/ trust economy really speaks to Millennials' idealism as a generation. They see a future—they're already living in a future— where this sort of system exists. Older generations are adapting to these ideas, but it's not who they are. The following four lifestyle themes make up the core of Millennials' identity:

1. Hyper-Socialization

Millennials are a connected generation, but it's more than technology that allows them to connect. They seem to love everybody: their parents, friends, and community. 82% of teenagers in 2005 (now Millennials in their late twenties) reported "no problem at all with any family member." This compares to 75% in 1983, and 48% in 1974.

We know Millennials are the "Friend" Generation. In our 2014 LifeCourse survey, 55% of Millennials agreed with the statement, "My friends are the most important thing in my life." This compares to 44% for Xers and 40% for Boomers. But it's not just about liking friends and family—it's about doing things together. Millennials like to work with others and collaborate in teams. In the world of videogaming, long thought of as a lonely geek activity, 72% of Millennials play with their friends or family members.

Perhaps the most telling event in recent media about Millennials' propensity for hyper-socialization and doing things together was the recent phenomenon called Twitch Plays Pokémon. Here's how it worked: An anonymous gamer from Australia developed a program on one of the world's most popular livestreaming sites for Millennials called Twitch.tv.

Every young boy knows Twitch; I mean every one. It has the fourth most kids during the course of a month than any other website in the world. Twitch is a place where a community can play video games together. Players can share their own gaming experience and watch people playing games all over the world. Kids can play a game with somebody in Sweden or Hong Kong. They can watch professional gamers, usually guys in their early twenties making $400,000 a year gaming all day long. Fifty million people watch Twitch during the course of a month. That's a bigger audience than network television. I like to call these kinds of jobs "avotainment." Avocation means job, and tainment refers to entertainment. More and more people are making a living in entertainment. Just as education and entertainment are merging, I think avocation and entertainment will as well.

On Twitch.tv, gamers input over 112 million commands to vote on how the main character should move. Together, they beat the game in sixteen days. Twitch Plays Pokémon is now a regular site feature where users play assorted Pokémon titles together. Furthermore, users have also enhanced the game in ways the creator could not have anticipated, from creating memes in photoshop to planning Pokémon battle strategies on social media. In essence, this one game created a thriving community of its own.

2. First Life/Second Life Blend

Millennials are the first generation that feels as much at home with their second life on the internet as their first life (their actual real life). IRL is a common acronym going around today—it stands for "in real life," as opposed to "life" on the internet. The fact that Millennials need to distinguish between the two suggests there would otherwise be confusion about which is which. This is a remarkable paradigm shift that can't be overstated.

Indeed, in the LifeCourse survey of young Millennials for MTV, 52% of Millennials think life is like a video game. Millennials trust technology. It was there with them in their crib and has always been a dependable partner. Millennials are likely to get deeper into interactive media, become even more engaged on the internet and in their second life, and (of course) bring their friends and family with them.

3. The Maker Movement

Like many new movements in the last few years, this one started with geeks in their basements. The whole Maker Culture represents learning by doing in a social environment. The Maker Movement is networked, informal, peer-led, and motivated by fun, learning, and achievement. This is quintessential Millennial! We know Millennials are highly networked to their peers, and we also know that the notion of achievement is very important to them. Good performance is a source of pride and social capital for Millennials, and the Maker Culture encourages both.

Millennials' time spent with user generated content (UGC) is up to 30%. This is content created by their friends and peers. In 2014, Disney purchased Maker Studios for a deal worth about $500 million. Microsoft introduced Project Spark to the gaming community, a program that allows players to create their own characters, plotlines, settings, etc. All these events point to a Maker Movement, and this has "Millennial" written all over it. As for the implications of the Maker Movement on media and entertainment, expect more Millennials to be using today's technology tools to advance their education and avocation. I predict that the entertainment industry will reshape the education business in America and throughout the world. After all, entertainers know better than anyone how to grab your attention and keep you engaged.

The Maker Movement has always been around but is getting quite big now. It started way back in the '50s with tinker toys and Legos: stuff you build with your hands you build with your hands. Millennials took this notion of making things and ran with it. (Remember Minecraft?) They're similar to the G.I. Generation; what did the G.I. Generation do? They built stuff: institutions, the education system, the government. With Millennials, this building will take place through the Maker Movement, and the Maker Movement is turning digital.

Remember the social networking site Myspace? Founded in 2003, it was very popular for Generation X. It was this dark place full of dangerous people; typical of Xer experiences. The sex trade got involved, and there were ads for drugs. When Facebook first came along, people were fearful; they didn't want a Myspace repeat. Society had learned that whenever people could connect online, bad things would happen. Of course, with Facebook, the opposite turned out to be true: an open, family-oriented environment was born. Then Instagram and Pinterest came out, which were creativity-based. Increasingly Millennials are spending their screen time looking at stuff their friends create.

4. The Barney Effect

The purple dinosaur millions of Millennials watched as children encouraged teamwork, cooperation, respect, and fairness. Whether it's support for same sex marriage or backing to reduce the income gap, Millennial values of equity, respect, and fairness were forged in their early years. Millennials are the first generation since the G.I.s to value a middle-class. 72% of Millennials believe the government should work hard to reduce the income gap between the rich and the poor, according to a 2014 CNN poll.

Along with this fairness and equity ethic comes Millennials' embrace for brands that have a socially conscious element. This notion of equity and fairness extends to expectations Millennials have of how products and brands are developed. This is often accomplished through crowdsourcing, which is second-nature to Millennials. Ben and Jerry's was one of the first companies to crowdsource flavors. According to the LifeCourse publication *Social Intelligence*, "Millennials expect brands to listen to their feedback and engage in two-way, interactive conversation with them." Wasn't it Barney who originally taught them to participate and share? Millennials feel it's important to have their voice heard in the decisions being made, whether it's an ice cream flavor or a privacy policy on Facebook.

Bringing Second Life to the Workplace Through Gamification

Young people are spending more time in second life than in first life, but the truth is that today, Twitter is real life. It's where you talk to your friends, share stories about your day-to-day life, and catch up with people you haven't socialized with in a while. This blending of first and second life is going to be magnified by virtual reality and augmented reality. When companies think about products and services, they need to think about how they place themselves in second life. How do they place themselves in virtual reality? How do they integrate their brand into the experience that people have when they do VR? How does Coca-Cola get their product into that medium? That's the stuff companies need to figure out to be successful among Millennials.

For a generation that grew up with Nintendo, PlayStation, and Xbox 360, it makes sense that Millennials seek out fun ways accomplish tasks and achieve goals at work. It is estimated that 70% of the largest companies today are using some form of gamification to attract and retain their young talent. Gamification applies game techniques to get people to achieve their goals. This is a $2.8 billion business. Think about it—Millennials have been conditioned to earn points, badges, or rewards through games or competitions. They like having targets set that are challenging but reachable with smaller goals along the way to measure progress and development. In addition, because Millennials prefer to compete as part of a team, forward-looking companies have found ways to use game techniques in a way that encourages collaboration, recognition, and support among employees of all ages.

According to Gartner Research, the gamification industry (primarily through apps and digital tools) will see significant growth in the next five years, with a market that could reach $5.5 billion. There are already numerous vendors that can help businesses use the concept; one of the best-known is a company called Badgeville. But many companies are developing their own models and internal competitions that promote productivity. One insurance company, Chicago-based Assurance, has started a Digital High-Five program that promotes positive public recognition and competition. Employees can give one another a digital high-five as a way to recognize good work. These are projected on LCD screens throughout the office for everyone to see. Employees "collect" high-fives, and each quarter the employee who accumulates the most wins an award.

Another insurance organization, Los Angeles-based Bolton and Company, hosted the "Bolton Rock Star Challenge." To promote creativity and collaboration among employees, the company asked employees to nominate each other. Nominees received a guitar pick, and the person who collected the most guitar picks at the end of a six-month period was proclaimed the winner. Gamification is one way employers can help Millennials see the link between what they do at work today and how it helps their professional development for meeting tomorrow's (or next year's) goals.

When it comes to work, VR has the potential to be really valuable. We could incorporate augmented reality and virtual reality with the notion of gamification to help Millennials develop. According to basic video game principles, there are four steps to any video game. There are rules, there's a problem, there's a solution to the problem, and there's typically a reward after you solve the problem: rule, problem, solution, reward. These four steps repeat themselves over and over again, whether it's Pokémon Go, first-person shooter games,

Minecraft, whatever you're playing. The more companies can incorporate that dynamic into the management of Millennials IRL, the better they're going to do. The companies that get behind this stuff are going to be the ones that are successful in the future.

Gamification integration in the workplace would make employees more engaged, and when they're more engaged, they're more productive. If you set a deadline for a goal, you could turn it into a gamification goal. As a manager, you could provide the rules of the game and the problem that needs solving, and push your employees to provide the solution with a reward at the end. Video games are a central part of many Millennials' lives. They have such a negative stigma, but in many games you actually learn. Consider Minecraft: it's very conceptual. For all we know, this game could be molding future city planners and architects and moral owners and community leaders.

The Quantified Self Movement

With this in mind, I believe in the future all education is going to be a combination of entertainment and education because it's the only way we can get Millennials to truly learn, and that's okay. It's not a bad thing to get people interested and excited about learning; that's what we want. Our education right now is based on a system that's 100 years old. It hasn't changed. I think we're headed for a radical renewal of the entire education system, and Millennials and their technology are going to be at the center of it.

For example, consider the quantified self movement, which is already in full-swing. The quantified self movement is an example of utilizing technology to track everything from daily mood to heartrate. FitBit, Daytum, Mood Panda—you'll be hearing a lot more about these self-monitoring devices that track your daily experiences. Apple is so convinced of the demand for these devices, they've developed an entire suite of Apps. Their new App, Digifit, is strapped onto your body to record your heartrate, pace, speed, and cadence of your running, cycling, and other athletic activity. Pricewater-houseCoopers has predicted that the worldwide market for mobile healthcare devices and communications will jump from $4.5 billion in 2013 to $23 billion in 2017.

Typical of emerging consumer movements, there are two generations at play: one that sets the conditions and one that adopts and consumes. Both Generation X and Millennials play a role here. Generation X was the first to embrace measurement as it relates to performance. Choice, behavior incentive, and market incentives defines this generation's contribution to the business world. While the Boomers were off accomplishing their "mission" (perhaps some ill-defined utopian state), Xers were quietly measuring the impact of activity on performance. Gen X Google founders Sergey Brin and Larry Page turned the advertising world upside down by introducing a pay-for-performance model of advertising. Now Xers have found a way to bring measurement and performance to personal human behavior. Most leaders in the quantified self-movement, first defined by Gary Wolf and Kevin Kelly in a 2007 *Wired Magazine* article, were born in the 1970s, while the consumers and enthusiasts were born in the 1980s and 1990s.

While early-wave Xers and Boomers may be wary of this self-monitoring, due to privacy concerns and technology adoption reluctance, Millennials can't wait to get their hands on this stuff. The culture of Millennials assures body-hacking is here to stay. Millennials are much more comfortable sharing their personal information over the web, so sharing even intimate details on sleep patterns is not a concern. Furthermore, we know Millennials are an achieving generation. They've grown up in an environment of measured goals. At the heart of self-monitoring devices is the ability to measure so you can improve. Millennials accept this challenge with gusto.

They've also grown up in a heavily monitored environment, so there is something comforting about the idea of monitoring their wellbeing. This was the first generation whose parents had listening devices in their room to hear every peep from the crib. Remember, Millennials trust technology. Technology is their friend. I can easily imagine a twenty-four-year-old posting her heartrate results on Facebook to the adoring comments from friends and parents: "Way to go!" This positive feedback, an essential motivator for Millennials, encourages better results, of course. And with their close relationship with parents, it is easy to see how texting results to their parents will be the norm.

Middleclass Millennials

Every generation is defined by their place in history and their coming-of-age experience. Millennials are known for their awareness of other people and their needs. You can't make a community great unless you understand who the community is. If you're a privileged white male and you don't understand the plight of a person of color who's in poverty and has been discriminated against all their life, then it's hard to build a community.

Millennials were the first generation since the G.I. Generation that fundamentally believed there should be a middle class and it should be bigger. We've gotten to the point where there's this huge bifurcation between people who make a lot of money and those who are very poor. The minimum wage in Virginia is $7.50 an hour. How can you possibly make a living on $7.50 an hour? I don't care what apartment you find and how many roommates kick in with rent and what discounted food you buy, that's almost impossible. This issue has been ignored for a long time, and Millennials are the generation that's going to start to pay attention to that, to figure out how we can create equity.

In terms of the workplace, Millennials expect equity and fairness, and if they don't see that, they're going to work to create it themselves. I'm the board chair at our church, and we're doing the Allyship workshop program to end racism. We're running into some conflict, and Boomers respond by saying, "It's leadership's fault, leadership needs to understand, and leadership needs to change their ways." All the Millennials involved counter, "Well, we can't do much by pointing fingers. Why don't we figure out how we get to a solution on this? Let's work collaboratively." It's an amazing generational divide I see every day. The oldest Millennial is only thirty-six.

Within the next ten years, they are going to be the policy-makers, and society is going to move towards more equity and fairness.

This idea points back to the participatory, prosocial economy; it all blends together. This is a community that's creating and sharing stuff, and that takes the power away from the few and brings it back to the many. ABC, CBS, and Time Warner are losing their grip. Corporations are losing their dominance over society. Thanks to Millennials, instead of three big companies in charge, now everybody's in charge. Here's the irony of it though: Google and Facebook have the power by giving people the power.

The Rise of Second-Wave Millennials

—— • ——

Just as you were starting to figure out how to manage
Millennials in the workplace, a major generational shift is
underway. Coming to a workplace near you: Second-Wave
Millennials.

Every generation has a first wave (older cohort) and a
second wave (younger cohort). Each wave has slightly different
traits because they were raised by the parents of two different
generations. Older Millennials are First-Wavers (as of 2018,
ages twenty-four to thirty-six) and were raised by Boomer
parents. Younger Millennials, coming into the workplace now,
are Second-Wave Millennials (ages fourteen to twenty-three)
and were raised by Generation X parents.

As an entire generation, Millennials have broad traits and
behaviors that are enduring and unique regardless of the
generation that raised them. But within these traits are subtle
differences based on how Boomers raised them compared
to how Xers raised them. These subtleties are apparent in
behavioral shifts in the workplace and include Second-Wave
Millennials' seeming lack of capabilities in written communications for the business world. In addition, face-to-face
communication coaching may be necessary to ensure Second-
Wave Millennials receive adequate training and development
regarding eye contact, posture, voice volume, and pace.

In addition, Second-Wave Millennials may have challenges in their ability to solve problems and think critically. Managers may need to provide training on problem-solving processes and tactics. Lastly, Second-Wave Millennials tend to have less self-awareness about their role as a team member in a workplace setting. Navigating their way as part of a team is often perplexing to them. But Second-Wave Millennials, despite these challenges in the workplace, can be developed into incredibly valuable employees. They will give their full loyalty and talent to your company if you simply invest in them.

Case in point: Samanthe has been at her new job for several days now. She's doing well, but she feels lost, like she's swimming in some vast pool with no walls to cling to. Luckily, they've started using Slack, which is her thing, but she still finds she lacks the coordination usually given to her by her superiors. Where are the cohesive instructions? Where's the roadmap and the user manual?

She glances up at the sea of computer screens, each employee bent to their own task. But she finished her task several minutes ago and still has two hours before the end of the workday. If she were Jennifer, perhaps she'd start playing solitaire at this point. Or text her husband. But she isn't Jennifer. She wants to go above and beyond in this business. She wants to *excel.*

On Slack, she sends her boss Zach an instant message. Even though his avatar says he's "away," she knows he'll see the message at some point:

Hey boss. All finished! U got any more wrk 4 me?
Zack responds right away: busy

Samanthe stares at the screen. Really, that's it? *Busy?* Like, he couldn't just tell her, "Check with Jennifer," or "File this report," or whatever? He had the two seconds to type out he was busy, but he couldn't bear to spend two more giving her directions?

Samanthe lets out a frustrated groan. Dave looks at her and frowns. He's on the phone but he mouths the words, *What's up?*

She shakes her head irritably, indicating it's all good. Then she sits at her desk while the interminable minutes tick by. She sits motionless, workless, directionless. And she does not like it. Needing something more to do, she goes through loads of possible avenues in her mind, but all of them finish abruptly at dead ends. Nope, she met that deadline already. Nope, Josh is working on the McKinsey & Company report. Nope, marketing never has anything she can do.

Ugh!

Samanthe gets up from her chair and goes to the breakroom. The refrigerator there is 100 years old, renowned the world over for its disgustingness. So, Samanthe takes some cleaners and rubber gloves from under the sink and goes about tackling her next project. She takes out the months-old rotten food people have forgotten about and throws it in the trash. Places all the food and drinks on a counter. Cleans the fridge inside and out, getting rid of some black gunk whose origin she cannot fathom. Partway through, with her hair falling in her face and paper towels, cleaning supplies, and food strewn about, she hears a familiar voice at the door.

"Sam … what in the world are you doing?"

She looks up. Zach.

"Hey, boss! Just cleaning. I didn't have any more tasks, so ..."

Zach sighs and rubs his temples. Samanthe immediately feels panic. "Oh, God, I'm so sorry ... I just, I didn't know what to do," she says breathlessly. "I—I ..."

"Sam," Zach says tiredly. "Relax, it's okay. It's not your fault, it's mine. Thank you for taking initiative. Once you finish this up come to my office, and I'll give you some tips for the next time I'm too busy to chat. Yeah?"

She raises an eyebrow. "I'm not ... in trouble?"

He laughs. "Of course not. It's my own fault. I didn't give you any direction. Man, Warren's going to love this."

Samanthe smiles. "Cool. Alright. Yeah."

Within fifteen minutes, she's finished her work and is sitting in Zach's office. He hands her a folder with extra work projects she can refer to if this happens again. She comes right back with, "Hey, what if I type all this up in a new Slack channel titled, "Extra Work," then whenever one of us runs out we don't need to scramble for new tasks."

Zach leans back in his chair and smiles. "Perfect."

Zach just followed one of the integral rules for Millennial coaching: he provided the Millennial direction. And she ran with it.

The Smartphone Divide

There are two main factors that cause there to be First and Second-Wave Millennials, number one being the introduction of the smartphone. It's kind of weird to think one innovation of technology could make such a difference, but it really did. It changed the way people think and interact. First-Wavers are the masters of technology, and Second-Wavers are the victims of technology. We relish in Millennials' understanding of technology, but what we haven't been talking about is the downside of technology on this generation. Second-Wavers were born starting in '95. The youngest would have been pre-toddlers when the iPhone came along. This exposure to technology came at a critical time in the development of these children and teens. It's going to have an impact for the rest of their lives.

Boomer Vs. Xer Parents

The second distinction between First and Second-Wave Millennials lies in those who were raised by Boomers and those who were raised by Xers. There's been a continuous progression in parenting towards even more overprotection, more coddling, more focus on achievement. Boomers are helicopter parents; there's no doubt about it. The Boomer parent is interested in raising a child who will turn out to be a great kid, but an Xer takes that a step further. An Xer parent is going to direct the steps that child must take in order to get to achieve. An Xer parent will arrange an interview at a private school when the child is four years old. Then they'll do more testing to figure out what the kid is good at. They'll finetune and hone the child. It's like breeding a horse. If they have long legs and endurance, let's get them involved in cross-country when they're five.

Desperate for Direction

If all your life you've been programmed in every detail in your life, then when you get to work, what can you do? You sit and wait to be told what the plan is. My wife has a Second-Wave Millennial intern working for her. She gave her an assignment to make a PowerPoint presentation and said she needed it in five days, by Tuesday. My wife waited and waited, and on Tuesday night, she asked the intern, "Did you do the Power-Point? I really needed it by Tuesday." The Second-Waver said, "Oh yeah, I finished it twenty minutes after you talked to me."

It was well done. My wife just never said, "Tell me when you're done with it." Without those instructions, the intern didn't know. The Second-Waver needs a blueprint. They need more structure. Guess who needs less structure? First-Wave Millennials and Xers. Second-Wave Millennials are closer in behavior to Homelanders. Before we know it, we're going to have a bunch of Homelanders coming into the workplace who are going to be an exaggerated version of Second-Wave Millennials, which is going to be problematic.

We know Millennials are collaborative and team-oriented. They're achievers; they're risk-averse. They value purpose and mission. They're bonded to their parents and friends. These are all broad Millennial characteristics. But whereas first-wave generations define themselves as leaders, Second-Wave Millennials seem to define themselves as followers, and that's not a bad thing. It sounds negative, but the reality is everybody has a place in society, and we need both leaders and followers. Besides, the best followers often become the best leaders. When I see Second-Wavers work in groups, they are amazingly collaborative, but no one's stepping up and taking charge of the group because no one wants to hurt feelings. Second-Wavers are much more cautious about emotions than First-Wavers.

Experience-Oriented

Further, whereas First-Wavers are goal-oriented, Second-Wavers are experience-oriented. First-Wavers are leaders; they want to accomplish their goal and get to the mission. With Second-Wavers, their parents have taught them that it's about the experience they go through, not necessarily the result. Consider the principle of meditation, a practice widely embraced by today's youth; it's not about the end-goal, it's about the experience.

First-Wavers have a bit more swagger in terms of their ability to be independent, but they're still collaborative. Second-Wavers often just sit and wait for someone to tell them what to do. This is the way they were taught in school. They're there waiting for leadership, and as a result, they become dependent on others. The percentage of parents who show up to job interviews of their kids has gone up. The college application process is usually done by parents. First-Wavers figured it out themselves, or their parents helped them. Now, for Second-Wavers, parents just handle things. This deeper parental involvement causes more dependency and less interdependence and independence. As a result, whereas First-Wavers tend to be street smart, Second-Wavers are more book smart. Improvisation is not their strong suit; they're more scripted. Their test scores continue to go up;

they learn what they study, but they don't learn much about real life.

Who Has the Time for a Job?

Fewer and fewer Second-Wavers are getting summer jobs because their parents want them to take extras courses over the summer so they can get even higher test scores. One of the great things about having a summer job is the learning that takes place. You learn how to interact with people. Instead of reading about people's emotions, you experience it. You learn about money. You learn about how hard it is to get up early in the morning. You learn about pay scales and about bad bosses and good bosses. Many Second-Wavers just don't get this kind of practical, hands-on experience, and it's partly because of these jetfighter parents whose focus is achievement, achievement, achievement—all through grades.

First-Wavers are more likely to look at the big picture, whereas Second-Wavers are more likely to look at the details. First-Wavers were trained to achieve at all costs, but that involves understanding the big picture. Boomer parents were every big picture-oriented: you've got to succeed in life, and you need to understand all the aspects of life in order to succeed. Second-Wavers are generally more narrowly-focused.

Success Through Wholeness

How they perceive success is different too. Success for First-Wavers entails reaching a goal and achieving something. Success for Second-Wavers involves this notion of wholeness. We're seeing this in schools now: the development of the whole child. It's not just about test scores. It's about the whole child: the level of empathy the child has and how they get along with other people. Social and emotional learning is getting to be a very big topic in schools. If you had a circle of First-Wave Millennials and you gave them a project and a goal, they would start working on the goal right away. The first thing Second-Wave Millennials would do is say, "How does everybody feel about that goal?" They'll learn about each other so they can understand how to best work together. Both are collaborative, but whereas First-Wavers focus on getting the job done, Second-Wavers want to understand each other as well. However, both groups will utilize one common tool. You guessed it: technology.

From Masters to Victims

In many ways, Millennials are the vanguard of today's revolutionary technology. When all these new digital platforms and social media forms came along, they mastered it. They were phenomenal. They created and owned all that technology. Unfortunately, because they're dependent by nature and because technology and social media are so powerful, Second-Wavers were sucked into it. Now they're victims of technology instead of masters. The goal of Facebook, Snapchat, Instagram, every website and app, is to get people to spend more time on their sites. They have sophisticated tools to accomplish this.

Born and raised in this world, Second-Wave Millennials are spending an unheard-of number of hours in front of their phones. For every minute they spend in front of their phones, it's one minute less they're out experiencing the real world. They're getting sucked into the second world, the digital world. This is a significant distinction between First and Second-Wave Millennials.

The Unprepared Second-Waver

One of the big reasons I became interested in generational studies in the first place was because my clients were telling me the people coming out of college over the last two years were very different, that they were less ready for work. They didn't have the soft skills. They weren't good communicators. They did not do appropriate follow-up after an interview. They were dependent.

Work is a scary place for Second-Wavers. They're not understood by older generations. It takes about five seconds for people to establish their opinion about someone. Let's say before she scored her new job, Samanthe went in for an interview with a Boomer. No one really told her what she should wear, so she comes in a little casual. It's summer, so she's wearing flipflops: strike one. The Boomer shakes Samanthe's hand, and Samanthe has the limp-fish handshake, which is the worst thing in the world to a Boomer. Boomers want a firm, strong handshake: strike two. She makes quick eye contact but then immediately looks the other way. The Boomer is used to someone saying, "It's nice to meet you." Samanthe never says that. She mumbles, "Oh, hi. Hi." Strike three. It only took ten seconds for the Boomer to decide Samanthe is no good.

She might not present herself very well in the way of posture, not standing tall and confident, but slouchy. When it comes to first impressions, these small physical things make a big difference. To humor her, the Boomer takes Samanthe back for the interview. He doesn't have a structured interview; it's something an Xer or a First-Wave Millennial might have, but not a Boomer.

"So, tell me a little about yourself," he says, smiling politely.

"Well, I grew up in Vienna, Virginia, and I went to school there my whole life." This is what she studied for, so she's detailed, specifically about her education. But she's probably very brief when she mentions her relevant experience because the fact is, she likely doesn't have much. The Boomer wants experience. He doesn't give a shit about education. He's been around for a while, and he's got a good poker face, but he's thinking, *God, this is going to be a short interview—I've got a lot of work to do, and this girl is not going to get the job done.* Samanthe might meet all the qualifications on paper; she might exceed the qualifications on paper. She has Excel skills, she has mechanical drawing skills, and she could probably do the job really well if supervised properly. But the Boomer has already decided he doesn't want this person. He doesn't want to have to babysit her.

Samanthe might say, "Can you tell me about the hours and benefits of this company?" Boomers and Xers hate to hear that in an interview because what that sounds like is, "I don't care about the job, I care about the benefits and the hours." No one coached Samanthe and told her not to ask that because she was busy studying for her SATs. She might say something like, "My parents asked me to ask about 401(k) and retirement benefits, the health plan, and if in the health plan you cover wellness." The Boomer is thinking, *I just want you to fucking do your job. You're talking about everything but work.* Samanthe wants to know where she'll fit in, which is legitimate, because if she's a happy employee, she's going to be a productive employee.

These Second-Wave Millennials are being cheated out of jobs because of who they are, and you know what? Companies are being cheated out of great employees. For example, manufacturing companies are really hurting for employees, so they're starting to recruit high school students for the work. Well, these kids are coming in and finishing their work so fast they have time to do their homework on the job; they're smoking these Boomers, and it's because it's a technology-based job, and Second-Wave Millennials are much faster and more proficient with technology.

Samanthe could be an awesome producer if only her interviewer recognized what it is she needs. The whole interview's a disaster, but that's usually what it's like to interview a Second-Waver: she's wondering why she should choose this job and how it benefits her personally, and the Boomer is wondering how she'll benefit the company. It's a stark conflict of expectations, and they've got to meet somewhere in the middle. The Boomer has to learn to understand the Second-Wave Millennial and her mindset because the reality is we're running out of Xers and First-Wavers to hire. We have to hire Second-Wave Millennials.

Second-Waver Strengths

A lot of the consulting work I do involves trying to explain to Boomers and Xers that the world is a different place than it was when they were looking for their first job. Young people today do not have the same values, attitudes, opinions, and behaviors that young people had fifty years ago. We have to adjust and welcome the new generations, because guess what? In the current state of the economy, you know who's in charge? The employee is in charge—not the company.

When a Second-Wave Millennial is told exactly what to do, and it involves technology in any way, she's going to run circles around everybody, including First-Wave Millennials. They're productivity machines. If you need someone to solve problems quickly and efficiently, there is no better generation than Second-Wave Millennials. Like First-Wavers, they're optimistic, positive, and collaborative. They understand team dynamics and consensus building. They're conflict adverse, so they're always figuring out ways to solve the problem. A Boomer will want to just stand his ground: I'm right and you're wrong. An Xer doesn't even want to get involved. Millennials, on the other hand, want to help solve the problem, especially Second-Wavers, who are in-tune with where everybody's coming from and what their emotions are.

If you are clear about what the roadmap is for your Second-Wave Millennials, what the goals are and how to get there, they will hit the deadlines. You just have to be specific and provide feedback. If you do that, they will do their job right. As an employer, it's your responsibility to provide a remediation training program that teaches them how to shake hands and practice good posture, dress appropriately, and speak wisely. If you teach it, they'll learn it; they're masters of learning. They'll be great employees if you just spend time with them and invest in them.

Communication is Key

Of course, if their job is to communicate regularly with clients, there could be some serious issues. Sure, they had to write papers in school, but when it came to communication, they've always used Facebook and Snapchat, not email or in-person conversation. The currency of the workplace (phone, email, and face-to-face) are not mediums they're familiar with. They just don't have enough experience with those things to know properly what to do, and that could get your company in a lot of trouble.

Millennials are authentic and open with who they are and what they do; they like to share. It's common for a Millennial to have spaghetti for lunch and then take a picture of it and send it around in the office captioned, "Spaghetti Day!" An Xer and a Boomer will look at that and say, "I don't give a shit what you had for lunch. Why are you showing me spaghetti?" It's part of a huge cultural shift. Millennials are willing to bring their personal life into their work life much more than other generations. That's true for both First and Second-Wavers, but it is a problem. When companies have only Millennials employed, it's not an issue because everybody's sharing everything.

A Millennial will feel comfortable sending a goofy picture of themselves and saying, "Me being goofy," because other Millennials understand; everybody's goofy. Human beings are goofy. For Xers and Boomers, there is no "goofy" in the workplace. There's a very clear line between work and life. Millennials don't see that line as much, and frankly, they want to work for a place where there is no line. Many companies have figured that out and done well recruiting productive Millennials. Other companies just haven't gotten it yet.

Accept, Adapt, and Educate

In many ways, Second-Wavers are simply not prepared for the workplace. Managers need to have an understanding of where these Millennials are coming from and how they got that way. They're not going to change; interviewers are just going to keep getting more and more of these kids. When you were coming into the job scene in the '70s, '80s, '90s, and early 2000s, it was different. Recognize this generation for what it is and be willing to spend time and money on remediation, training, and skill-development to help these young people get acclimated to the workplace.

Leaders and managers aren't ready to do that. They want the ready-made employee. But Second-Wave Millennials need time, they need acculturation, they need skill-development. They need, need, need, and a lot of managers scoff at that. Yes, these kids are dependent, but you know what? You're not going to make them less dependent by yelling at them and telling them they're wrong. You can't tough love them into working harder. Take a step back. Get to know the Second-Wavers, find out what makes them tick. Put them in classes, bring in training companies, and focus on developing them. If you don't, you may never get them to be productive.

Put Yourself in Samanthe's Shoes

Second-Wave Millennials face a workplace that's still stuck in the 1990s. The communication style is old-fashioned, the technology usually isn't up to speed, the office itself is old, and the managers learned how to manage from a book that came out forty years ago. It's hard for Second-Wavers. They can't communicate well with their boss and colleagues. They want to know the exact steps to accomplish the tasks at hand, and they want to know what their next job in the company will be. They want to know how working here actually contributes to the skill-development they need to have a fulfilling life. All too often in companies, that information just isn't available, and the path isn't defined.

It's challenging because they're used to things being laid out for them, and suddenly everything is unclear. Now they don't know what to do. They can't not have a job, but they're not going to take initiative, so they're just stuck being unproductive employees. That's why it's so important for all generations to gain knowledge about one another. Then we can develop plans to bring them together and create a more productive workforce. What you want is engagement and retention. When a Second-Waver leaves your company after six months, then you have to put up an ad, interview new candidates, and go through the whole process again. That's expensive, and it takes a lot of time. You want people to stay at a company as long as possible. As a company, you need to figure out ways to engage these Second-Wavers to keep them where they are.

The Millennial Hierarchy of Needs

——— • ———

Care — *Is somone looking out for me?*

Direction — *How do I achieve my career and life goals?*

Purpose — *Wait! why am I doing this, anyway?*

Feedback — *How do I know if I'm on the right track?*

Structure — *What are the rules of the game?*

We've talked about who Millennials are and their impact in the workplace. Now it's time to get into the specifics of what they need in order to be the best employees around. I work on the topic of generations, specifically Millennials, every day, and I was never able to figure out a coherent way to tell managers what these Millennials need and how to manage them. Finally I got to thinking, there's got to be a hierarchy for managers so they know where to start.

The hierarchy of needs helps identify the most significant things you can do as a manager, supervisor, boss, etc. It explains the most important needs of Millennials and the things you can do to address those needs and foster a productive workplace. I thought Maslow's hierarchy of needs was a good model to use to help people understand this. The elements of this pyramid have changed many times as I've tried different techniques out, and now it's finally perfect.

Structure

At the very bottom of the pyramid is structure. The most important thing you can do with Millennials, particularly Second-Wave Millennials, is be clear about what their job is and what the rules are. Millennials do know how to read, so go beyond the job description and talk to your Millennials about exactly how they should behave in the workplace. Structure is so important for Millennials because it's always been very much a part of their lives. Xers and Boomers never had much structure, so when they got to the workplace, they didn't expect structure. They expected to figure it out themselves, but Millennials want a more comprehensive view of things.

At Gallup, we designed a model that was tested by 800,000 managers; there was a huge amount of data behind it. Basically, we came up with the twelve conditions necessary in the workplace for people to be engaged. The very first item is simply the statement, "I know what is expected of me at work." Remarkably, something like 50% of employees out of the five million we interviewed didn't completely agree with that statement. In other words, 50% of employees running around doing their jobs don't agree that they know what's expected of them. That's a recipe for disaster; it means they're not engaged, and when employees aren't engaged, work can be done really poorly.

Second-Wave Millennials have a gravitation towards protection and control: rules are important to them. The students who survived the Parkland, Florida shooting are extremely vocal. Well, what they're really saying is that we need more order, more structure. "If we had rules, these things wouldn't happen." If you don't establish structure for your Millennial employees, nothing else matters. It's kind of the "food, water, and shelter" of the hierarchy of needs: the fundamental starting point.

Feedback

Next on the pyramid is feedback. Feedback is an important element for Millennials, and again, amplified for Second-Wave Millennials. In their coming-of-age experience, they received feedback on almost everything. It's not just feedback that's important for them in the workplace, it's frequency of feedback, which needs to be very high. It's not enough to give feedback once a year in a performance review. It's not enough to sit down on a quarterly basis, every three months. It's not even enough to sit down with your Second-Wave Millennial employees once a week. This makes many managers cringe, but the fact is that you probably need to do it every day. Ask them how they're doing and talk about your expectations; it only needs to take a couple of minutes.

Consider this: Some schools have done away with textbooks and now only use iPads. Everyone in the school has an iPad, and there are no pencils or pens. When they do homework, they get feedback electronically almost instantaneously. What happens when you do a Google search? You get the information immediately. Millennials don't know anything else.

Purpose

If you're a manager and you provide clear structure and frequent feedback, you're going to have a Millennial employee who's pumped to go to work—but something will still be missing, and that's the third element up the pyramid, which is purpose. Millennials will always ask, "Wait a minute, why am I doing this? What purpose will I serve?" This is a generation that grew up with the highest volunteer rates of any generation: they value helping others, buying food that's ecofriendly, stuff like that. Millennials want their job to serve the community, serve some larger purpose. A manager's role is to emphasize the link between their personal purpose as an employee, and the purpose of the organization. One distinction I've noticed about Second-Wave Millennials is that many want to put purpose at the bottom of the pyramid—that is the most essential element of their needs. Indeed, not every Millennial sees the order of the hierarchy in the exact order, but all agree on the five core elements.

Let's say you have a Second-Waver in the insurance industry. It's their first job out of college, and they're happy to get a job, but it's kind of boring. A typical manager would say, "Okay, here's your job. This is what you do." But what really helps is to instead say, "Let me tell you about the insurance industry. It actually saves lives. It helps build houses for people whose houses have been destroyed; it's a vital part of the economy. You're helping and protecting people." Be clear that their role serves a larger purpose.

Direction

Then we move on to direction. I'm talking about professional development, guidance in how your employees can achieve their career and life goals. They expect their manager to be a mentor and a coach. Invest in them. In structure, you've established the ground rules. In feedback, you've established the frequency and mode of communication between you and your Millennial. You understand them enough to know what their interests and values are. When it comes to direction, a great manager will sit down and spend time with their Millennial employees, helping them think through the direction they're going in their job and in their long-term career. Great managers will help Millennial employees create a map. Millennials have long-term time horizons. They were trained by their parents to think about the future. Helping Millennials with their direction is very important to their development. It gives them confidence and trust in their manager. Think of yourself as a guidance counselor.

Don't wait six months to work on direction. Do it almost immediately, during orientation or within the first couple of weeks when the Millennial arrives in the workplace. They need this; older generations didn't. Think about Boomers. Boomers were hostile towards authority figures. If an authority figure gave a Boomer a map and promised them a nice life with a picket fence and two kids, the Boomers wanted the opposite of that. When Xers came along, authority figures didn't even think of providing that because they were worn down by the Boomers.

It's totally different with Millennials. They've been inspected, prodded, directed, put into car seats, told to refine their soccer skills so they would perform better. They were given detailed syllabi in school. When they get to the workplace, they expect this to continue. A lot of older managers have a problem with this because they see it as handholding. The reality is, managers need to make the time for it because they're going to get a better return on investment.

Care

The need at the very top of the pyramid is something only the best managers do. Those who do it end up not only getting the best performance out of their employees, but they're more likely to retain that employee in the long-term. As a result, they save the company a lot of money. At the very top of the pyramid is care. Direction is about professional development, and care is about personal development. Care means taking an emotional and genuine interest in the wellbeing of your employees. Don't look at their career like they're some cog in a machine. What you really want to do is dig deep and develop relationships.

I was having a conversation with a manufacturing company in Houston, and the guy I was talking to was managing a group of Millennials. He was telling me about one Millennial who always came into meetings on time, but within about forty minutes he would always fall asleep. "How could he possibly do that?" the manager asked me.

"Instead of saying, 'You can't do that,' find out why the heck it's happening," I said. "Ask him."

It turned out that a couple of months earlier, the Millennial's mom was diagnosed with cancer, and he and his sister were taking turns staying up late helping with the chemo and doing hospital visits. Every behavior has a root cause, and simple care gets at what that root cause is. A manager simply saying, "I'm sorry for what you're going through," provides the Millennial with confidence and trust in that manager and allows them to perform at higher levels. It makes them more motivated to work because they have what they believe to be a positive, trusting relationship with their manager. That's care. A happy employee is a good employee, and you don't make your employees happy with ping-pong tables and latte machines, you make them happy with care. It's easy to buy a ping-pong table, but the fact is that your employees need more than that. Relationships are what matter most.

Customization

An important question for managers to ask themselves is how they can customize the experience for their new employees. Millennials have been raised to expect an individualized experience in almost everything they do. When I was growing up, there were three television channels. Fifteen years later, there were about 500. Now there are as many channels and media options as there are Millennials: millions. In the past, if you wanted information, you'd go to an encyclopedia or ask an expert, and you may not get exactly what you want, but you got pretty close. Millennials have a totally different experience with knowledge and information than other generations; it's all personalized to them.

THE MILLENNIAL HIERARCHY OF NEEDS | 181

There was a groundbreaking book written about twenty years ago by Don Peppers and Martha Rogers called *The One to One Future*. It talked about how the consumer market will be moving from mass marketing to a world where every product and service will be customized to the individual. It turned out to be a prophetic book. iPhones have a million different colors to choose from. 3D printing machines can craft things that are specific to the needs of the person making the request. How does this notion of customization translate to management structure in the workplace?

Let's use praise an example. Some people like to be rewarded for good work by having an email sent out about them, so everybody knows they did the job they were supposed to do. Other people love to achieve their goals, but they don't want to make a big fuss about it. As a manager, it's important you understand that every person you manage is different. Older managers resist this because when they were young everyone was rewarded the same way. Well, Millennials are different. They expect a more customized experience.

Android's slogan really captures the Millennial way of thinking: "Be together, not the same." Millennials like to do things together and within a community, but they don't like to be exactly like the person next to them; they want to be special. As a manager, you need to think about how you can create a customized, special experience for your Millennial because that's what they're used to. That's their frame of reference. Some managers will throw a party to celebrate someone's birthday or their work success, but not every employee wants all that attention. Maybe someone is shy, and they'd be embarrassed to get up and give a speech. That's very different from managing in the past, when everything was generalized.

People use "snowflake" to describe Millennials because all snowflakes are different. The reality is, everybody is different and everybody's always been different. It's important to harness those differences for the good of the company and the individual. That's what this is all about: making managers more effective at their jobs and making employees more effective. Every manager has a responsibility to attend to this hierarchy of needs.

Parents at Work

Fostering a sense of community was never all that important before Millennials, but now it's crucial, and this is a hard one for managers to grasp. I've done consulting for the US Air Force, and many of the airmen are under a lot of stress. Most are not actively serving, but they're very busy and living in a place that's not home, that's away from their community. Because technology has allowed Millennials to stay in touch with people, they've developed a community of friends, and if they're in a different place, they really miss that and want to develop their own community. Senior officers (or managers in the workplace) need to think about how to help soldiers connect more with their community. How can you help your airmen connect with their friends back home and make new friends? Millennials spend twice as much time with their parents growing up as their parents spent with their parents. In other words, the amount of time I spent with my parents, as an Xer, was half the time I now spend with my own Millennial children.

Typically, there's a very strong bond between Millennials and their parents, and they want to keep that bond going. When Millennials were entering schools, teachers realized parents were going be part of the child no matter what: they couldn't get the parent out of their office, so they ultimately had to accept that the parent was an important part of the student. So they figured out how to work together with the parents, as a team, to make Sarah the perfect student. Well, the same should go for employers. Employers need to realize that parents are an important part of these Millennials' lives. Any way you can connect the family with the company is going to be a positive step.

A number of companies (Facebook, LinkedIn, Hewlett-Packard) have "bring your parent to work day." Everybody laughs when I tell them that, but why? The parents will come because they want to know where their kid works. Just because your parents didn't want to see where you worked when you were growing up doesn't mean Millennials' parents don't. Connect the parents. Connect the friends. Reward Millennials for referring their friends to the company. I can imagine a number of positives coming from involving the community. When the parent or family builds up an association with their child's work, if the child were to say, "Man, work is annoying me. I'm thinking about quitting," maybe the parent would be more involved and say, "Why don't you talk to your boss about it before making any rash decisions? I think Fred would really like to hear you out on this one."

Inescapable Community

Glassdoor is a website most Millennials look at when they're evaluating companies. It's a window into the culture of an organization. They read reviews from actual employees about what it's like to work there. This terrifies companies. If employees are having a bad experience within their work community, all the Millennials are going to know about it.

There are many ways for managers to establish a positive community within the workplace. It's helpful if a company has a relationship with a charitable foundation or nonprofit in the community. A company in California has an event every single weekend: a fundraiser, a 5K run, a bake sale, whatever. They publicize it on social media, so there are always events and activities available to Millennials. When you're in the community representing your company, that's a direct hit. That's exactly how you bring community to the organization. Millennials are taking leadership roles in these foundations: They're organizing fundraisers and raising money, which creates a stronger bond with the company. It's kind of ironic that by creating more work for the Millennial, it makes them more engaged in your company. That's the magic of having something meaningful for them to do; it allows them to connect.

WeWork

WeWork is a radical concept a couple of Gen Xers came up with. They realized that if they created an open office space with reliable Wi-Fi and free lunch, startups will just come and rent the space. When that happens, other startups come and rent the space too, and then all those startups can communicate and learn from each other. They become a community of their own. Basically, what WeWork is doing is taking real estate and making it into a community. WeWork has a market capitalization of billions of dollars, and all they do is rent office space and supply food. The idea is very attractive for Millennials because they can cohabitate with organizations unlike their own. They learn from each other, and maybe they'll start another business together. In this community, people can't wait to go to work because they don't know which interesting people they'll meet today in the common area.

This is perfect for Millennials, but it would not have worked with other generations. I'm a member of the Tower Club in the Washington, D.C. area. It's an exclusive club where a lot of CEOs belong. Our space can be used for meetings, to invite clients for lunch, events, etc. I think that model is going to die away to be replaced with more things like WeWork. In the Tower Club, there's a dress code, and the lunch menu is heavy and expensive. Sometimes I just want a wrap or something simple. I don't want to spend nineteen dollars on a salad. Millennials are very money-conscious; WeWork is perfect for them in a multitude of ways.

Future Factory

The Massachusetts Institute of Technology (MIT) Lab is a space created for exceptionally smart people to work on anything from prosthetics to robotics. The crazier the project, the better. They put all these high-IQ folks together, and amazing things happen. Companies like General Electric are investing in this space, and that's all it is: space. It's just square footage. It really supports the notion of Millennials' interest in community. I expect some of the greatest innovations of our time to come out of the MIT Innovation Lab and similar places that fuel Millennial creativity. If I were a writer sitting next to a doctor, we're very different. Getting into conversation, maybe I'd realize a concept for a medical thriller that I wouldn't have ordinarily thought of because I wouldn't have spoken to a doctor.

Millennials have discovered the value of connection and community more than the generations before them, and most people don't realize that. They look at Millennials and they see entitled, needy, clueless kids. What they're not seeing are the positive traits Millennials bring that are very different than their own, the progress they're fostering. But it's there. It's happening with WeWork. It's happening at the Innovation Lab. It's happening all over the world. And the companies that understand and embrace that are the companies that are going take us to the future.

Listen to Your Millennials

In most speeches I give and meetings I go to, I mention Slack. It's a remarkable tool used mostly by Millennials, but there's an enormous generational divide. I was at a Fortune 100 company in Washington the other day in their Technology Department. I brought up Slack, and all the older tech guys rolled their eyes. "Yeah, yeah. The Millennials all want to do that, but they don't realize how dangerous it is." I could see the seething frustration of the Millennials, who knew they could get their job done so much more efficiently if they used Slack. It's for communication and productivity. I see Slack as a Facebook-meets-project-management software. It's a platform to connect with the people working with you and congratulate them if they do a good job on something. It also has IM-ing, so you don't have to waste time writing long emails. There are so many elements to Slack representational of the Millennial Generation that older generations don't understand. This is our future.

Slack and programs like it give new meaning to the "workplace." Older generations assume "community" indicates a physical "place," which it can, but Millennials have expanded their thinking about place and community. They have brought their community into the digital world. It's easy for Millennials to slip into a conversation with people around the world about a subject people around the world are interested in. If you're really interested in tenth-century agriculture, guess what? There's someone else somewhere in the world who's also interested in that, and they're probably not next door. They may be in Sweden. Well, no problem—you can easily connect with them, and boom, there's a community.

Coaching is the New Managing in the Workplace

———— • ————

When you're a mentor, you really are a coach. You should be spending time getting to know your Millennial. Think about the Millennial hierarchy of needs: structure, feedback, purpose, direction, care. A good coach focuses on direction and guidance, and a great coach cares very much about the Millennial.

I'd like to differentiate between managing and coaching. A manager manages your performance, and a coach manages your development. While a manager sets your goals, tracks your performance, gives you raises, promotes you, fires you (very functional things), what a coach does is motivates you. They provide feedback. They fit you into a team. They improve your skills. They give you advice. It's a one-on-one experience. A manager is more removed and hierarchical. Coaching is focused on developing the person. Coaching is the new managing for Millennials. Here's why:

Millennials grew up to believe they were special. When they enter the workforce, how will they respond to someone who doesn't treat them that way? A distant authority figure doling out unexplained assignments and lofty goals without explaining how to get to those goals is not the way to develop good employees. On the other hand, someone who will work closely with them, mentoring and partnering, coaching them to better performance, will experience far greater levels of productivity.

The word "management" conjures up a faceless bureaucratic infrastructure, at worst malevolent, and at best indiscriminate: rule-making and decision-making at its worst. Peter Drucker said, "So much of what we call management consists of making it difficult for people to work."

Let me clarify. The principles of good management still need to apply: clear expectations, a means of tracking progress, and rewards for achieving goals. But how a manager manages, especially for Millennials, should be more like a coach—developing his or her employee with close supervision and a watchful, caring eye.

Old habits die hard, and if you've been a manager for more than ten years, I can understand the inclination to subscribe to the philosophy, "If it ain't broke, don't fix it." But something does not have to be broken in order to fix it. Change happens, and the strong are those who can adapt. Millennials are different from the previous two generations. They are the change that is happening in the workplace, and coaching, not managing, might be the change that gets your organization to higher levels of productivity. Take it from Drucker when he says, "If you want to start doing something new, stop doing something old."

Give 'em Goals

Millennials in the workplace are far more goal-oriented than their Boomer and Gen X counterparts. You may be thinking that Millennials are starry-eyed dreamers, but that was actually the Boomer generation when they were young. Or maybe you're thinking Millennials are slackers, just drifting to and fro, but that was Xers when they were young. Of the three generations currently in the workforce, Millennials are decidedly the most focused "on the prize."

What Not to Do

Managers need to exercise caution to avoid irreversible errors in managing this generation. Turnover remains high with Millennials, but research still suggests that they would rather work for "one perfect employer" than hop from job to job. So here are five don'ts for managing Millennials and helping you keep them around as long as possible.

Don't: Practice Tough Love

Most middle managers and even senior managers fall into the Generation X (ages thirty-six to fifty-six) category. Xers came of age at a time of economic malaise and cultural tension. For them growing up, the world was a dangerous place. Unwanted pregnancies reached a peak in the US in the '80s and early '90s, and drinking and driving and drug-use increased. While Boomers practiced "free love," Xers worried about AIDS. Because of their gritty experiences, Xers entered the workforce fairly successfully on their own with no help from anyone. They were the survivalists and entrepreneurs who embraced risk with a fiercely independent spirit. I see many Xer managers treat Millennials with the kind of tough love mentality they experienced when they entered the workforce. News flash:

Millennials don't "get" tough love. Their experience was entirely different growing up. They were raised carefully by their helicopter parents, who surrounded them with teams of teachers, counselors, physicians, and tutors who worked on every aspect of their development. Their expectation for the workplace is the same. You can't give a Millennial too much attention.

Don't: Give them the Big Picture on an Assignment Without Details

As empowered and confident as Millennials are, they need descriptions of assignments in detailed clarity, especially Second-Wave Millennials. It is not enough to say, "Read through this 1,000-page document and create a three-page summary." You need to identify for them exactly how the summary should be developed, what font and format you want, when you want it by, and what resources are available to help them complete the assignment.

Don't: Take Away Their Toys

A few years ago, I was doing a research project for a US government agency. We were trying to identify the drivers of satisfaction among Millennials. While the top results all had to do with feedback, two elements emerged that were unexpected: they wanted larger monitors or even two monitors on their desks, and they wanted to be plugged into to their social network throughout the workday. I realize there are some jobs where this would not be possible, but consider the two things that have always been a priority for Millennials: cutting-edge technology and the ability to connect to their social network. A hotel manager in Germany told me, "I tried to stop them from getting on Facebook, but it was impossible. Instead, I have designated times for Facebook breaks throughout the day, and this really has helped, not hurt, productivity and morale."

Don't: Assume They Don't Care about Benefits

One of the most remarkable and unexpected characteristics of Millennials is their interest in benefits like 401(k), retirement, health benefits, wellness and flex programs, etc. It was always assumed that young people don't care about these things—after all, retirement is a long way off, and young people are generally healthy, but according to a study by MetLife, this does not appear to be the case. In fact, Millennials value benefits even more than older generations do. There is also emerging evidence that Millennials are investing a higher percentage of their income into 401(k)s compared to older generations. So don't assume Millennials don't care about these issues, and make sure you provide plenty of opportunities to explain these benefits in great detail.

Don't: Try to be "Cool" Like Them

This is an awful strategy. Millennials expect older generations to act their age. Millennials already have a very positive and informal relationship with authority figures, and they share many cultural interests with their parents. But Millennials value interactions with their own generation. Don't insert yourself into their friend network and start posting stuff on

Facebook, Twitter, and Snapchat. If you do, you will not be cool; you will be weird, and you just might chase your Millennials away.

What Are Soft Skills, and Why Don't Second-Wave Millennials Have Them?

It is said that hard skills get you hired, but soft skills get you fired. What's the difference? Learning an obscure component within an agile software development process is a hard skill, but holding a fork properly at a client dinner where you are clearly explaining the obscure component is a soft skill. Having a certification in SSL, Java, or BASIC are hard skills, but convincing your boss of an idea in person while making eye contact is a soft skill. Get the drift?

Increasingly, Second-Wave Millennials are entering the workplace book smart but not street smart. There are really two reasons for this: one has to do with parenting and the second has to do with technology. Together they're making a perfect storm for a soft skill crisis in the workplace. In fact, alarms have been raised by so many employers I talk to that I started a company called Second Wave Learning to address the soft skill gap for these Second Wavers. I encourage you to check us out at www.secondwavelearning.com. In the meantime, the next few pages are a little cheat sheet on the skills you should be teaching them.

But back to why soft skills are lacking: GenX parents (the jetfighter parents) have perfected the path their kids must follow in order to get good grades, high test scores, and access to the best colleges. Their kids' schedules are so over-prescribed—particularly with academics—that there is little room for anything else. There is no "free time," and on the weekends young people are being tutored or participating in scheduled sports instead of having a job at 7-Eleven or the hardware store. Their inexperience with part-time jobs through high school and college makes their first "career" job much more challenging.

Even jobs at home, a.k.a. "chores", have decreased. Research by Whirlpool concluded that just 28% of parents regularly assign chores for their kids, even though 82% say they grew up doing chores themselves. And, in the meantime, parents are not introducing the basic soft skills, like how to introduce yourself to an adult, enunciating clearly, or proper etiquette at the dinner table.

When Second-Wave Millennials do have free time, they usually spend it in front of a screen, and this is the second reason they are lacking soft skills. More time in front of a screen means less time in front of people. Messaging replaced texting, texting replaced email, email replaced phone calls, and phone calls replaced good old-fashioned face-to-face communication. In his book, *The Shallows*, Nicholas Carr makes a case that adolescents' increased interaction with technology is actually changing the neuroplasticity of their brain. The problem is compounded as multinational companies, like Facebook, identify ways to keep people addicted to their devices. All of this takes these Second-Wave Millennials away from the development of interpersonal skills.

So, there is this huge gap between what is learned in school and what is practiced in the workplace. And it is exacerbated by parenting and technology. Employers had never thought of themselves as the remediators of soft skills. Their training departments are not set up to do this, and there is a feeling of resentment among older generations about these new hires coming in without having these basic soft skills. The most common question I hear among older generations is, "How come we knew how to do it, and they don't?" Hopefully, the previous few paragraphs answered that question. In a nutshell, the answer is, "You were raised in a different way, and at a different time." Ergo, the generation gap!

Oral Communication

There are many ways of communication that come and go, but communicating by voice is something that will probably never go away, and it's something Second-Wavers don't have a lot of experience in. Talking is simply not something they do a lot of. I've been at companies in Silicon Valley where the workplace is about 80% Millennial, and you can hear a pin drop in a room full of forty people working. No one is verbally talking to each other. They communicate in their own ways, usually digital, but they're not talking. The reality is, when you get into interacting with clients and partners and collaborators in a business, you're going to have to learn how to speak.

They need training in this regard, and it's up to the manager to provide that. Ideally, a company would have training sessions on public speaking, and a camera would tape the new employee. There's nothing scarier than watching yourself on tape, but it helps you be a better speaker. It helps with clarity, diction, posture, what to do with your hands. These

196 | S<small>ECOND</small>-W<small>AVE</small> M<small>ILLENNIALS</small>

are things many Second-Wave Millennials were simply never taught.

Written Communication

Written communication has undergone immense change within just the last ten years. You may notice this when you get emails from Second-Wave Millennials. Oftentimes, sentences start with words that are not capitalized. There are typically run-on sentences and misplaced commas. There's essentially no grammar. In Snapchat and Twitter and all the other digital ways Millennials communicate, grammar isn't required to understand what someone is telling you. But in the workplace, Xers and Boomers have very specific ideas about the way writing should be.

Second-Wave Millennials need soft skill training on how to use proper grammar and how to write a business proposal, stuff like that, because there's an expectation in the workplace that they can do these things. Second-Wave Millennials' brand suffers if they don't do these things. They come off looking stupid, and they're not stupid. We know Second-Wavers are smart. It's not a question of intelligence, but it is a question of norms and expectations of older generations in the workplace.

Presentation Skills

One of the other things I've noticed about Second-Wave Millennials is their inability to make eye contact when they're talking to you. There's nothing that drives a Boomer (or an Xer, or a Silent Generation, or sometimes a First-Wave Millennial) crazier than a young person who doesn't make eye contact, who shuffles their feet when they talk and looks to the side. They simply haven't been told what to do by their parents. It's not a subject in school, so they're not learning about presentation skills. Presentation skills are about organizing your thoughts and crafting a message in a way your audience will understand. We know they're good at that because on Snapchat, they can tell a whole story without any words. They're remarkably creative, they just have different ways of communicating. It's up to employers to make sure these Second-Wave Millennials learn of other ways of presenting themselves that may be more direct for their older coworkers and clients.

Collaboration

The next key to training Second-Wave Millennials is collaboration. Young people are naturally team-oriented. They're comfortable being on a team, but they may not know exactly where they fit into that team, and oftentimes they wait for instructions. It's important we teach them that if there is no apparent leader on the team, it's okay for them to step up and take charge; in fact, it's great. It's necessary. We need to help these Second-Wave Millennial employees understand that it is okay to be clear about their strengths and tell people what they think.

When I think about collaboration, I think about emotional intelligence, or EQ. Emotional intelligence is the ability to read the emotions of others. We are now teaching it in our Second Wave Learning course called **Slay the Job**^{SM} with the intention to give these newly-minted hires the ability to recognize people's emotions and respond to them respectfully. The more in-tune they are with the emotions of the people around them, the more successful they're going to be in collaborative environments and their job in general. Many studies suggest that emotional intelligence is even more important than IQ when it comes to success in a career or relationship. The good news is that it can be taught, and that's why it should be part of soft skills training for these young people. Group dynamics and consensus building are all about working on a team and reading people's emotions.

Problem-Solving

Young people know how to solve problems. They did well in their classes. But in a work environment, it's a little different. As an employee, you have to identify what your priorities are. If you have a job as an account executive at a company, you've got to figure out what you spend your time doing and what you focus on because you want to spend more time on the things that are priorities for you. If your priorities are to get new accounts, you're going to want to make sure to spend time identifying the accounts that you'd like to secure and doing research on them, actually setting up appointments and meeting with them to procure those accounts. Problem-solving involves doing research and developing a plan, and Millennials need some training in this regard.

Hire in Teams

To nurture teamwork from the very beginning, companies should hire Second-Wave Millennials in teams. I talked to a company in Chicago that only hires new employees (between five and ten) every six months at exactly the same time so they start on the same day and do orientation and training together as a group. This way, the new employees develop a common identity. There's a certain bond they form through team-building sessions and group events. From the very beginning, this company is nurturing the culture of teamwork. The United States Army has done a program for several years called the Army Buddy Team Enlistment Program. It lets friends enlist at the same time as one another. A recruitment center is a scary place, but if you're going to be with your friends, it's a lot different. If you can go through training with a team by your side, it becomes easier, and there are higher levels of engagement. Nurturing teamwork is critical.

Consider not only hiring in teams, but compensating in teams. Restructure the compensation program so that people get bonuses for team achievements. Everybody in your team has their own salary, but when there's a successful group project, everybody on the team might get a 3% bonus or gift certificates to Starbucks or something.

It's also important to look at the physical environment of your office space. Are you an office that has individual cubicles, or are you an office that has open spaces and common areas? Most Millennials prefer open spaces and common areas, and these spaces encourage the teamwork that's so critical to success. Isolated working spaces stifle teamwork and hinder productivity. That's one of the reasons places like WeWork are so successful among Millennials.

Foster a Millennial-Friendly Culture

Create a positive environment at work. Foster a can-do attitude, an optimistic culture. Encourage positive reinforcement and rewards for accomplishments. A lot of managers hate the idea of giving Millennials VIP treatment, assuming the tough love approach is the best way. A tough love approach just doesn't work. If you have a competitive, dog-eat-dog environment, Millennials will not want to be there.

There are all kinds of ways to increase positivity. Millennials often see life in terms of a video game, which a lot of people think is scary, but it's really not so scary. Remember, there are four parts to a video game: rules, problem, solution, reward. This applies very easily to the workplace. Tell your Millennial what the solutions are in order to address a problem. Then, when they achieve the goal, they get a gift certificate to Target or a virtual star. It's that simple.

The company in Chicago I mentioned earlier: They have flat screens all over their offices and when an employee feels that another employee has done something awesome, however small, they can go onto this instant messaging board and post, "Emily hit her goals today!" and it gets posted all over those TVs. What you end up with is this growing amount of information that's all positive. It makes people feel like they're in a community, and they're accomplishing something great.

The decision to implement these programs is the role of the leaders of the organization. Leaders hold the keys to what the culture is at an organization. And leaders need to understand that Millennials gravitate towards a positive work environment. It's not that older generations don't like positive work environments. I think everybody does, but Millennials are extra sensitive to that and are more likely to leave a company if the environment isn't positive enough.

One Week Later

——— • ———

Maybe you've learned that generations are far more complex and significant than you realized. Generational differences play a huge role in the workplace, and I hope this book has armed you with some knowledge that can prove useful in managing a more productive workplace, being a more helpful employee, and just being more understanding of the people around you. There are a number of very simple things you can do to better coexist with people of all ages and generally be more patient, engaged, and satisfied with your peers, family, and coworkers.

I've been hanging out with Josh, Samanthe, Dave, and Jennifer for the past week. I've seen ways in which they can get along, but they falter due to their own generational make-ups. And, time after time, I've homed in on these differences, bringing them to light to shed understanding. So what if Sam doesn't type out emails or Slack messages using proper grammar? She's not working for the editorial department of some publishing company, she's in sales support, and she does a masterful job at it. She's so young and driven, she will only get better.

Yes, Dave is mortified by new technology, but that doesn't mean he should throw in the towel and quit, or worse, get fired over it. He requires patience and understanding, and maybe even a few ego-boosts for good measure. This is exactly the type of help a Second-Waver can provide. Jennifer is apathetic, but she does a good job. She's entrepreneurial at heart and, using her Gen X survival instincts, she can often spot trends before they happen.

Josh wants to succeed just as badly as Samanthe, and being older, he's in a position to take on a management role sooner than her. Sure, he talks a lot, and he desires to work with a company that practices some form of positive intention, but can you blame him? Let him be himself, and give him the roadmap to achieve his dreams.

As with every new spate of hires, bugs need to be worked out, but all in all Zach's got a great team here. If he can utilize just an ounce of the lessons imparted in this book, he will be on the path to powerful coaching, leadership, and a more fundamentally successful business enterprise. Equipped with a team like this, each member of which has their own unique quirks and capabilities to drive the vision forward, there is no reason this can't be done.

———— • ————

On my last day, I stride across the linoleum of the familiar conference room in front of Zach and his employees. They're smiling now, in stark contrast to my first day, when they seemed confused and out of place. Samanthe, in just a single week, has proven herself a highly intelligent and fast-learning asset to the business. Josh and Dave went out for a beer last night at the local sports bar, where Josh listened to his elder talk about kids and grandkids for over an hour. He didn't interrupt once. Jennifer and Sam are texting outside of work, with Sam offering to babysit Jen's kids so her and her husband can go on holiday to the south of France. They're a patchwork irony. Opposing forces now going in the same direction, and getting along.

I couldn't be prouder.

"Always remember," I conclude, "that you're not all as different as you look. There are some differences, of course, but if you can harness these differences and learn to work with them, not against them, you guys will be virtually unstoppable. The next age of business is not a whitewashed room with people wearing the same outfit and acting the same as everyone else. It'll be an old man in a suit sitting next to a young woman in a punk rock tee-shirt and jeans. They'll belong to different generations and will possess very dissimilar coming-of-age experiences. They will talk and act differently. They will learn differently. But they will follow the same set of rules. And they will accept each other as they are."

Jennifer stands to return to work, but when she glances at Samanthe, for the first time she sees her own daughter with her uncertain eyes and kind, optimistic demeanor. Jennifer had raised her daughter carefully, in hopes she would grow up to be compassionate and successful, but mostly just happy. She realizes Samanthe's parents, likely Jennifer's age, probably raised her with the same goals in mind.

As Samanthe heads for the door, Dave lifts his arm to stop her. Her heart sinks, but then Dave smiles. "You're doing a great job, kid," he says.

"So are you," Samanthe says with a smile.

Dave's eyebrows raise in surprise, and he begins to laugh. Quietly at first, then steadily growing louder. I hurry to sling my bag over my shoulder and slip past them into the hall, eager for the combined laughter of a Boomer and a Second-Wave Millennial to mark the end of a successful training course and the beginning of a productive workplace. Sky's the limit.

Endnotes

——— • ———

Introducing the Generational Divide

"Age." U.S. Bureau of Labor Statistics. Last modified August 30, 2018. https://www.bls.gov/cps/demographics.htm#age.

Gallup, Inc. 2018. "The Engaged Workplace." Gallup.com. https://www.gallup.com/services/190118/engaged-workplace.aspx.

"Lifecourse Associates, News Article: 'Across The Generations.'" n.d. Lifecourse Associates: What Is a Generation? https://www.lifecourse.com/media/articles/lib/2012/0221201 2.html.

Gallup, Inc. "The Engaged Workplace." Gallup.com. https://www.gallup.com/services/190118/engaged-workplace.aspx.

Coffman, Curt W., and Kathie Sorensen. *Culture Eats Strategy for Lunch: the Secret of Extraordinary Results, Igniting the Passion Within.* Denver, CO: Liang Addison Press, 2013.

Field, Mary Blitzer. 2003. HRDQ: *What's My Leadership Style?* HRDQ.

Why Generations Matter

William Strauss and Neil Howe. *Generations: The History of Americas Future, 1584 to 2069.* New York: William Morrow, 1991.

Isaacson, Walter. T*he Innovators: How a Group of Hackers, Geniuses, and Geeks Created the Digital Revolution.* New York: Simon & Schuster Paperbacks, 2015.

"Strauss–Howe Generational Theory." Wikipedia. Last modified August 30, 2018. https://en.wikipedia.org/wiki/Strauss–Howe_generational_theory.

Douglas Coupland. *Generation X: Tales for an Accelerated Culture.* London: Abacus, 1991.

"Post–World War II Economic Expansion." Wikipedia. Last modified August 23, 2018. https://en.wikipedia.org/wiki/Post–World_War_II_economic_expansion.

"Morbidity and Mortality Weekly Report (MMWR)." Centers for Disease Control and Prevention. Last modified November 22, 2017. https://www.cdc.gov/mmwr/volumes/66/ss/ss6624a1.htm?s_cid=ss6624a1_w.

Corporation for National Community Service, Volunteer Rates. https://www.nationalservice.gov/pdf/06_1203_volunteer_growth_factsheet.pdf. (2018).

Strauss, William, and Neil Howe. 1998. *The Fourth Turning: an American Prophecy.* New York: Broadway Books.

Cox, Amanda. 2014. "How Birth Year Influences Political Views." *The New York Times.* July 7, 2014. https://www.nytimes.com/interactive/2014/07/08/upshot/how-the-year-you-were-born-influences-your-politics.html.

Baby Boomers: "My Way or the Highway"

"GDP and Other Major NIPA Series, 1929–2012:II"
https://apps.bea.gov/scb/pdf/2012/08%20August/0812%20g
dp-other%20nipa_series.pdf

"UCLA Freshman Survey." 2018. HERI.
https://heri.ucla.edu/cirp-freshman-survey/.

Generation X: "Just Do It"

"Mortgage Rates History." 2018. United States Prime Rate.
http://www.fedprimerate.com/mortgage_rates.htm.

DeStefano, Anthony M. "NYC Homicide Rate Lowest since
WWII, Stats Show." A New York. Last modified January 5,
2018. https://www.amny.com/news/nyc-homicides-record-
low-1.15725051.

"Behavioral Risk Factor Surveillance System." Centers for
Disease Control and Prevention. Last modified September 4,
2018. https://www.cdc.gov/brfss/index.html.

Howe, Neil. 2014. "Generations In Pursuit of the American
Dream." http://ttp://www.lifecourse.com/assets/files/
reports/Generations%20in%20Pursuit%20of%20the%20
American%20Dream.pdf

Sawyer, MD, Susan M. 2018. "The Age of Adolescence."
Lancet Medical Journal. https://www.thelancet.com/
journals/lanchi/article/PIIS2352-4642%2818%2930022-
1/fulltext

Millennials: "Friend Me"

Frey, William H. "The US Will Become 'Minority White' in 2045, Census Projects." Brookings. Last modified September 10, 2018. https://www.brookings.edu/blog/the-avenue/2018/03/14/the-us-will-become-minority-white-in-2045-census-projects/.

Fry, Richard, Ruth Igielnik, and Eileen Patten. "How Millennials Today Compare with Their Grandparents 50 Years Ago." Pew Research Center. Last modified March 16, 2018. http://www.pewresearch.org/fact-tank/2018/03/16/how-millennials-compare-with-their-grandparents/.

"Why Our IQ Levels Are Higher than Our Grandparents with James Flynn." Ted Talks Psychology, Last modified May 10, 2015. http://tedtalkspsychology.com/james-flynn-why-our-iq-levels-are-higher-than-our-grandparents/. Center for Disease Control, Suicide rate, https://www.cdc.gov/vitalsigns/suicide/index.html

Center for Disease Control, Suicide rate. https://www.cdc.gov/vitalsigns/suicide/index.html

"Lifecourse Associates, News Article: 'Teenage Volunteers Give Team Effort.'" Lifecourse Associates: What Is a Generation? https://www.lifecourse.com/media/articles/lib/2002/031402-mjs.html.

"Teens Who Spend Less Time in Front of Screens Are Happier - up to a Point, New Research Shows." The Washington Post. Last modified January 22, 2018. https://www.washingtonpost.com/news/inspired-life/wp/2018/01/22/teens-who-spend-less-time-in-front-of-screens-are-happier-up-to-a-point-new-research-shows/?utm_term=.b8df04723911.

Global Workplace Analytics. n.d. "-2018 Alternative Workplace Strategies Fifth Biennial Benchmarking Study." Global Workplace Analytics. http://globalworkplaceanalytics.com/telecommuting-statistics.

Smith, Aaron. "U.S. Smartphone Use in 2015." Pew Research Center: Internet, Science & Tech, Last modified April 1, 2015. http://www.pewinternet.org/2015/04/01/us-smartphone-use-in-2015/.

"Millennials as Digital Natives: Myths & Realities." 2018. Nielsen Norman Group. https://www.nngroup.com/articles/millennials-digital-natives/.

"Myths, Exaggerations and Uncomfortable Truths." 2018. IBM IX | Your Business by Design Partner. May 9, 2018. https://www-935.ibm.com/services/us/gbs/thoughtleadership/millennialworkplace/.

"Indeed Survey: Graduates Optimistic About Job Prospects." 2018. Indeed Press Room. http://press.indeed.com/press/indeed-survey-graduates-optimistic-about-job-prospects/.

Gallup, Inc. 2016. "What Millennials Want From Work and Life." Gallup.com. May 10, 2016. https://www.gallup.com/workplace/236477/millennials-work-life.aspx.

Landrum, Sarah. 2015. "Why Flexible Working Hours Make Employees More Productive." Inc.com. October 15, 2015. https://www.inc.com/women-2/why-flexible-working-hours-actually-makes-employees-more-productive.html.

Hiring and Managing Millennials

Quast, Lisa. 2012. "How Becoming A Mentor Can Boost Your Career." *Forbes Magazine.* August 21, 2012. https://www.forbes.com/sites/lisaquast/2011/10/31/how-becoming-a-mentor-can-boost-your-career/#3f4139d55f57.

"Lifecourse Associates: Finding Three." n.d. Lifecourse Associates: What Is a Generation? http://www.lifecourse.com/services/generations-in-the-workforce/white-paper/findings-lib/finding-three.html.

Landrum, Sarah. 2015. "Why Flexible Working Hours Make Employees More Productive." Inc.com. October 15, 2015. https://www.inc.com/women-2/why-flexible-working-hours-actually-makes-employees-more-productive.html.

Beck, Julia. 2017. "How Some Companies Are Making Child Care Less Stressful for Their Employees." *Harvard Business Review.* July 19, 2017. https://hbr.org/2017/04/how-some-companies-are-making-child-care-less-stressful-for-their-employees.

"High Growth Industry ProfileHealth Care." n.d. History and Fitzgerald Act, Employment & Training Administration (ETA) - U.S. Department of Labor. https://www.doleta.gov/brg/indprof/healthcare_profile.cfm.

"Reports." 2016. CEW Georgetown. July 12, 2016. https://cew.georgetown.edu/publications/reports/.

"Employee Tenure News Release." 2016. U.S. Bureau of Labor Statistics. U.S. Bureau of Labor Statistics. June 30, 2016. https://www.bls.gov/news.release/archives/tenure_09182014.htm.

"Millennial Survey 2018 | Deloitte | Social Impact, Innovation." 2018. Deloitte United States. August 23, 2018. https://www2.deloitte.com/global/en/pages/about-deloitte/articles/millennialsurvey.html.

"Millennial Generation Survey Report". Griffith Insurance Education Foundation. https://www.theinstitutes.org/doc/Millennial-Generation-Survey-Report.pdf

"GR:14 Ethics | Deloitte | Global Services, Integrity, Ethical Principles." 2018. Deloitte United States. June 29, 2018. https://www2.deloitte.com/us/en/pages/about-deloitte/articles/gr14-ethics.html.

"Why Generations Matter." Lifecourse Associates: http://www.lifecourse.com/assets/files/Why%20Generations%20Matter%20LifeCourse%20Associates%20Feb%202012.pdf.

Geiger, Abigail. 2018. "How Americans Have Viewed Government Surveillance and Privacy since Snowden Leaks." Pew Research Center. June 4, 2018. http://www.pewresearch.org/fact-tank/2018/06/04/how-americans-have-viewed-government-surveillance-and-privacy-since-snowden-leaks/.

Millennial Lifestyle Themes

Surowiecki, James. *The Wisdom of Crowds: Why the Many Are Smarter than the Few.* (London: Abacus, 2014).

LifeCourse, Relationship with Friends. 2018. "Understanding: Life Domains." n.d. Charting the LifeCourse™. https://www.lifecoursetools.com/principles/understanding-life-domains/.

"Can Business and Government Meet Millennials' Expectations?" 2014. CNN. Cable News Network. January 22, 2014. http://globalpublicsquare.blogs.cnn.com/2014/01/22/can-business-and-government-meet-millennials-expectations/.

"Gamification 2020: What Is the Future of Gamification?" 2012. Gartner IT Glossary. Gartner, Inc. November 5, 2012. https://www.gartner.com/doc/2226015/gamification-future-gamification.

The Rise of Second-Wave Millennials

The Millennial Hierarchy of Needs.
"Gallup Employee Engagement Center." n.d. Gallup Q12 Employee Engagement Center. https://q12.gallup.com/Public/en-us/Features.

Peppers, Don, and Martha Rogers. *The One to One Future: Building Business Relationships One Customer at a Time.* New York: Currency Doubleday, 1997.

Coaching is the New Managing in the Workplace

European CEO, Peter Drucker, "A History of Peter Drucker and His Impact on Management Theory." n.d. European CEO. https://www.europeanceo.com/business-and-management/a-history-of-peter-drucker-and-his-impact-on-management-theory/.

"Broker and Consultant Trends" n.d. MetLife Employee Benefit Trends Study. https://benefittrends.metlife.com/.

"Research Indicates Sparing the Chores, Spoils Children and Their Future Selves - The Boston Globe." 2015.

BostonGlobe.com. The Boston Globe. December 8, 2015. https://www.bostonglobe.com/lifestyle/2015/12/08/research-indicates-sparing-chores-spoils-children-and-their-future-selves/ZLvMznpC5btmHtNRXXhNFJ/story.html.

About the Author

Warren Wright is Founder and CEO of Second Wave Learning, a talent development firm that helps companies attract and retain Second-Wave Millennials. Their signature program, Slay the Job^{SM}, teaches soft skills, emotional intelligence, and generational collaboration in order to create more intention and awareness among all employees. He keynotes frequently at conferences, corporate events, and companies about the impact of generations in the workplace and society at large.

Warren is a First-Wave GenXer and has worked as a sales-person, manager, and executive in radio and TV, survey research, strategic consulting, and leadership development, as well as several start-ups. He lives in Northern Virginia with his wife, and has two First-Wave Millennials.

31178905R10130

Made in the USA
Middletown, DE
29 December 2018